How to Write an Exceptional Business Plan

*A Step-by-Step Guide to Winning
Investors, Lenders, and Success*

ASHLEY CHEEKS, MBA

LUCIDBOOKS

How to Write an Exceptional Business Plan
A Step-by-Step Guide to Winning Investors, Lenders, and Success

Published by Lucid Books in Houston, TX
www.LucidBooksPublishing.com

ISBN-10: 1-63296-368-X
ISBN-13: 978-1-63296-368-0
eISBN-10: 1-63296-381-7
eISBN-13: 978-1-63296-381-9

Special Sales: Most Lucid Books titles are available in special quantity discounts. Custom imprinting or excerpting can also be done to fit special needs. Contact Lucid Books at Info@LucidBooksPublishing.com.

I cannot explain how deeply grateful I am for the support of my husband and children for their unwavering encouragement and positive energy through this process.

Elliott, Jordyn, and Michael, I dedicate this book to you. Thank you for being such amazing human beings. You three are the rock solid foundation for everything I do!

Table of Contents

The Set for Success Template Kit

Most templates range anywhere from 20 to 45 pages of instructions—and those instructions say NOTHING about how to create financial projections.

This template kit is different.

A companion to this book, your template kit includes:

- Pre-built charts and tables
- Pre-formatted style and layout
- Pre-written headers and section titles
- Pre-itemized tips and instructions in each section for quick reference
- Pre-design conforming to the Written Success professional standard for fundraising

Plus, this template kit includes a financials template that auto-creates charts, forecasts, and key financial statements for you.

The template kit provides a framework that has strategic formatting and tactics throughout—everything from the font choice to the spacing to the margins are all designed for maximum readability and modern, sleek, professional appearance.

This kit will save you hours of work, give you seriously important shortcuts and easy secrets on what to put where to impress any bank, partner, or investor audience, and help you write an exceptional business plan quickly.

writtensuccess.co/template

Special Thanks

I want to thank each of the contributors who endured interviews, phone calls, and really honest and raw discussions about the realities of entrepreneurship in order to make this book a useful tool for other entrepreneurs. Not only did each of you bring a unique perspective that others will greatly benefit from, but you brought openness and candor that made this book more real than I ever could have achieved alone.

Thank you, Rob and Lacey Britton. You have a beautiful focus on what matters most in life, and your purpose-driven path to create a great life for your family will make you successful in all you do. I am grateful that you shared your journey and am excited for all that is ahead for you!

Thank you, Billy Rinchin. You have a story that is already riddled with moments that would have broken a lesser person. Your unwavering dedication continues to propel you to great success. I am grateful that you allowed me to see a piece of your story and am so appreciative that you continue to share your gifts with the world.

Thank you, Milo Cavalcante and Omar Lynn. Your infectious, positive energy and powerful focus on amplifying your ideas are second only to your humility and servant spirits. As serial entrepreneurs, you have only scratched the surface of what you will achieve, and I am grateful that you have opened your hearts in honest ways that always leave people better off than they were before they knew you.

Thank you, Paul Roberson. Your amazing desire to create communities and celebrate commonalities will result in a business that makes more than a product; it will make a real impact. I was moved by your interest in creating connections and am so grateful that you are willing to be a trailblazer for those in your life and beyond who need to see you succeed in order to believe they can achieve their dreams, too.

Thank you, Mark Lewis. Your ability to balance passion with practicality is unbelievably powerful, and on behalf of small business owners everywhere, thank you for using those qualities to create a business that helps others in a very real way. You have many gifts, and I am so grateful that you are laser-focused on using them to benefit others in the most impactful way possible.

Thank you, Travis Rypkema and Josh Brazier. You embody what a great partnership can do for a business and what a foundation of genuine friendship can do to add real power to any vision. I am unbelievably grateful for your sharing the rawness of your journey and can't wait to see what the universe has in store for you next.

Thank you, Rob Harmon. You live for more than your own needs, and I have undying respect for your mission to personally increase health, happiness, and community in this world through your vision. You have more than mere goals; you have an ideology that will allow people to engage and maximize their lives in holistic ways. I am so grateful for your loyalty to your purpose, which will benefit so many people in truly life-changing ways.

Thank you, Philip Agostini and Edwin German. Your solution for making a global impact not only in people's lives but also in the sustainability of our world is one that could only be created by beautiful hearts and brilliant minds such as yours. I am so grateful for your diligence in making this concept a reality and am so excited for what's ahead.

Thank you, Ishmel Sanchez. Your perspective and mentor-driven approach in supporting the growth of entrepreneurs is incredibly rare, and I have so much respect for your genuine interest in their success. You've reached a level where your insights are invaluable, and yet you act selflessly to share them with anyone who may benefit. I am so grateful for your generous spirit and your respect for what it takes to achieve true success.

Thank you, Corbin Cook. You have a mix of integrity, intelligence, creativity, and analytical spirit that has the power to create empires. It never ceases to amaze and inspire me when you share your new ideas and brilliant insights! I am so grateful and honored to collaborate with you and am excited to support your continued success.

Thank you, Aatif. With your amazing gifts and desire for continuous improvement, you are someone I learn from with every conversation. Your modesty is unparalleled despite your credentials and experiences, and I cannot express enough how grateful I am to have you as a supporter and friend.

Preface

Most entrepreneurs let fear drive them down the wrong path. That is especially true if they feel fear of failure or fear of falling short of someone else's expectations. If you are afraid to let your loved ones down or to be judged by family or friends, then you might feel a ton of pressure to make this work.

If you know you need an investor or a bank loan, you may also feel fear about not getting the money you need. You may be especially fearful of doing something wrong that would jeopardize your funding, like not writing a good business plan.

In order to feel more comfortable, many entrepreneurs write long and detailed business plans that make them feel good, as if a *longer* plan is the same as a *better* plan. They get lost in the weeds and buried in the details, and they completely lose sight of the point of the business plan.

I did this when I first started. My business plan was written and rewritten over and over, revised and extended, added to and elaborated on. Along the way, I lost my own focus and ended up creating a rambling encyclopedia instead of an actionable, effective business plan.

I worked on that business plan from a place of fear. I was afraid it would flop, afraid my business idea wouldn't work and that my family would suffer because of my bad business plan. I was afraid to be seen as a failure in their eyes. I was afraid they would see that I had no idea what I was really doing.

For me, and for many other entrepreneurs, the biggest problem with inexperienced business plan writing is knowing what to write and where to stop. Understanding how much is enough and exactly what to put in each section can help you breeze through your business plan. Then, you can actually use that plan to work on your business. After all, that is where the *real* journey begins.

Your business plan is more than just a document. It is a piece of a bigger decision to grow your own business. With that decision comes a ton of uncertainty. Up to this point, there have been plenty of periods in your life where you have questioned your decisions and circumstances. You may remember moments when you didn't know whether you could make ends meet before your next paycheck or whether you would be able to find a place to stay during hard times. There were times when you felt completely lost and maybe a bit hopeless, not sure when things would turn around for you.

I am here to help you work through those feelings during this phase. I've felt lost more than a few times both before and after my entrepreneurial journey began. As I ventured out to build my own business, I felt like there were no answers to be found. I felt like I was alone. There was a constant pressure to avoid failure, to prove that I could make this work. During it all, I found myself lost, not quite sure if what I was doing was right or wrong. As I launched my business, I also remember feeling like I had zero control of what would happen next.

In the end, I did lose my way—more than once and with more than one business plan. After failing a few times and seeing where I went wrong, I finally began creating my own success. Eventually, my business plan matched my business potential.

You might wonder how likely it is that you are starting your own business story successfully. You might get the sense that by executing your business plan, you are about to start something big, something life-changing. You might also wonder if you'll have enough money to survive this next phase or if you will be smart enough to make the right decisions along the way.

How to Get Out of the Weeds and Focused on an Effective Business Plan

This remarkable time will have an extraordinary impact on your future. The way you build your business plan will either translate into clear action or complete confusion. In order to create a useful plan, you need to know your goal. Then you need to know how to create a business plan that pivots with you when your goal moves a bit. Because chances are, your goal will grow, and not in ways you may be able to predict right now.

I'm not only going to share my own guidance, but I'll also share bits of valuable guidance from others who have found unique paths toward success. This is important because knowing all the ways you can succeed is usually more helpful than focusing on all the ways you can fail.

Because you are reading this book, you are already on your way to building a business that is destined for success—one that will afford you a life of personal freedom. I wonder if you have ever noticed how easy it is to read a how-to book that has real-world examples. You might have already realized that you can finish a technical book more quickly when you imagine how it directly applies to you.

In this book, you will discover a step-by-step guide to writing a business plan. You will see how each step is based on real-life examples of business plans I finished for some of my most amazing clients. You will see how those clients were in the same stage you are in right now and how they used certain approaches to move toward success in their own businesses. This is a practical guide that is designed to focus your attention only on what matters so you can finish your business plan smoothly.

Along the way, I'll also tell you the truth about key moments in my personal journey with some of these business plans. The goal is to show you more than just *what* to do to finish your business plan. Instead, you will come away from this book with a new way to think about key components of your business.

Ready to Get Started?

The next section will help you get your core documents handy and ready for the process of building your business plan. In the Introduction, you will read about the flow of this book and the rhythm you can expect. You will also read about the expected length of your final business plan if you use the template files that are included with your copy of this book. Finally, you will find out what to have ready before you write page 1: your Appendix and References.

Introduction

Rhythm, Templates, Appendices, References

Throughout this book, you will get step-by-step guidance on how to complete each section of your business plan. Because there are different ways to approach each section, I focus on the simplest ways that are easiest to finish while creating maximum impact.

In this introduction, I will briefly explain the rhythm you can expect the book to follow. You will then read about how to use this book with the templates provided. After that, I will show you how to prepare the content for your Appendix and References pages so you can keep them updated easily throughout your business plan build-out.

Rhythm

The rhythm of this book is very deliberate in order to maximize your time and minimize your effort. Each chapter will introduce you to someone in the entrepreneur space. Most are at the business plan moment of their journey. Several of them are clients I have supported, and sharing a piece of what was needed to finish their business plan will help you work through how you can finish yours with a bit less headache.

Each chapter will also include additional insights that will be helpful if you are using your business plan for something specific such as an investor, a bank loan, or strategy clarity. These tips will also give you a shortcut for how to update your business plan quickly. For example, if you are preparing to send your business plan to a bank for a loan but you get an offer of interest from an investor, you can quickly update your business plan to be investor-ready with a few specific tweaks based on advice offered in each section.

If you are interested in investor funding, you will also see in each chapter considerations for creating a great impact for investors. Tips will include what the investor will look for and things to keep in mind if you are building your plan for investor fund-raising. In the end, you will have clarity on how each section of your business plan can best cater to investor review.

On the other hand, you may be hoping to use your business plan to secure a bank loan. Each chapter also includes advice and considerations for scenarios when you are seeking a bank loan. Tips include what to think about while building your plan for underwriters and areas to be mindful of while you write your content and create your financials.

If you are building your business plan to clarify your own strategy, you will notice that each chapter includes a special callout for what to consider. Each chapter will help you stay focused and will guide you toward a concrete, executable strategy. Once finished, your business plan will be a clear road map to success for your business vision.

The explanation of how to complete each section of your business plan will be the heart of each chapter, which includes images and examples where applicable. The information is practical and will steer you away from noncritical items. Your time will be focused on building the most impactful parts of your business plan.

Each chapter ends with a few things you need to avoid so you don't fall prey to common pitfalls. Each chapter also includes an example of a finished business plan excerpt and a quick recap of how I finished a client's business plan. That will help you envision your own ending and get to it faster.

Templates

This book comes with a preformatted business plan template and a financials template. It is organized in the order of the template provided, with the exception of the References and Appendices. It is important to keep notes in your References section from the very start of your business plan effort. It is also important that you stay aware of which Appendix items are important while you work through putting everything together.

These two sections are critical. When business plans are too long or include too much information in the main portion, they simply become too difficult to read. It may seem ironic, but bank underwriters and investors dread seeing a long business plan. They have just as low of an attention threshold as the rest of us. When a teacher assigns a 10-page homework assignment, its purpose is for you to master the topic. The teacher is looking for key concepts and indicators that you mastered the material. However, that doesn't mean the teacher *wants* to sift through 300 pages of summaries from her students. She will glaze over from time to time, lose interest, and get frustrated when it appears the students didn't put their best efforts into the assignment. After a while, the assignments will run together and all seem like white noise in her memory.

Your banker or investor audience knows you need to finish a business plan in large part to simply benefit your own knowledge. They also know that you put a lot of time and effort into your plan. When you are able to take all of that and condense it to just the core components, it makes your plan more readable and more memorable, and it shows that you clearly know your stuff when it comes to your business.

For this reason, the main business plan should only be about 20–25 pages long, including financials. Anything longer than that risks losing the attention of anyone who reads it. Before we get started with your core business plan, let's see how to spot items that best belong in the Appendix and when to add things to your References section.

Appendices

Your Appendix (or Appendices) section allows you to include everything you see as important in your business planning efforts. There will be a lot of useful information you want to have in your business plan, but not all of it will fit or make sense in the main sections of your document. Adding too much content to the main part of your business plan can be simply overwhelming.

Table of Contents

Example Table of Contents with Appendices

Help your reader by adding bulky things to your Appendix. That can include the following:

- trademark or patent documents
- architectural or product drawings
- drafts of menus
- brochures or marketing materials
- samples of logos in progress
- additional market research you found interesting
- quotes or estimates gathered for start-up costs
- full-page, high-resolution images

Try to create one Appendix page per topic or item and give each Appendix a line in your Table of Contents as shown in the image to the right. As you work through your business plan, keep a folder on your computer of any items you plan to add to your Appendices when your business plan effort is complete. As you research and gather estimates for costs and forecasting, you may find at the end of this journey that you have a few new items you want to include later in your final plan.

References
Your business plan will include a lot of external effort. When you find demographics for a zip code, you may not remember if the figures you used in your plan came from zillow.com, city-data.com, or the United States Census Bureau, for example. Simply listing where data sources were found will help you go back later and quickly get access to the facts you found.

References also create a quick way for investors and underwriters to check your research.

It is helpful to include a simple in-text reference that aligns with the first couple of pieces of information from your References section. Then your audience can easily go back and consider the source of your information.

References add credibility to your business plan. They also save you from being unprepared for the dreaded question, "Where did you get that information from?"

The City of Houston's population is 2,349,993 (City-Data.com, 2020). Based on this estimate and assuming 1% conversion on the upcoming marketing campaign, just over $20,000 for equipment purchases will be needed to move operations in a scaled direction. Most capital expenditures will be recorded as assets and depreciated. The balance of the asking amount will support payroll costs and operational costs during a time when new projects are awarded, but milestone payments are expected after project costs are incurred.

Example In-text Citation

References

Houston, Texas. (2018). *City-Data.com.* Retrieved from http://www.city-data.com/city/Houston-Texas.html

Planning & development demographics. (n.d.). *City of Houston, Texas.* Retrieved from https://www.houstontx.gov/planning/Demographics/

Example References Page

I recommend you use a format that feels quick and easy for you. I use a modification of APA style references, but if it's easier, you can simply list the URL where you found the information. Whatever allows you to simply and easily keep a list of your sources, adopt that style and keep your References page handy throughout your business plan effort.

How to Get Started

This is it—this is where the business plan begins! To get started, we will review the Executive Summary and how to build it. As you go through all the chapters, keep your business plan template handy and complete each piece of your plan as guided.

Chapter 1

Executive Summary

*Life felt like a grind to me, with the work and
commuting and never feeling like I was quite happy.
But I do like to live life on the safe side,
with a stable paycheck and such.
Then one day Rob asked me, "Why not do something else?
Why settle for a job you're not happy with?
Why not live your best life?"*

—Lacey Britton and Rob Britton,
founders of The Vine House

www.vinehousebedandbreakfast.com

THE VINE HOUSE
Bed & Breakfast

W hen Rob Britton, CFA, and Lacey Britton, MBA, first contacted me to finish their business plan, they already had a fantastic business plan in place. They had drafted their plan on their own, and to this day, I still remember how impressed I was with all the brilliant work they had put into their business plan. There was a ton of research, great competitive landscaping, and lots of operational strategy that truly blew me away with its depth and accuracy. I did, however, see where attention was needed on page 1 of their business plan to make it absolutely perfect.

They were opening a bed and breakfast called The Vine House in Temecula, California. It was located in the heart of wine country, which was ideal for this tourist-friendly business. Lacey's human resources background and her five-star AirBNB hosting experience, coupled with Rob's experience in business and finance, literally painted the image of a power couple in the making. Their partnership was perfect for launching this business. Lacey had a natural talent for design and customer service, and she structured most of the business vision and process strategy. Rob brought his strength in numbers and business savvy, and together, they created a partnership balance that most entrepreneurs can only dream about.

To launch their business, they needed a Small-Business-Administration-ready business plan to secure a loan for more than a million dollars. They had already bought the land; now they needed to create the building. Their excitement and passion were tangible, and I clearly saw that they were ready for this venture. They had no hesitation that they would make this dream a reality.

When I reviewed the draft of their initial business plan, I felt a burden to get it just right. I already knew that the problems I normally face in business plan development wouldn't apply here. There was nothing wrong with the research, the numbers were conservative and reasonable, and the launch strategy was solid. The burden I felt was presenting this perfectly. I knew that if everything wasn't laid out in a strategic way from the first page turn, then the underwriting team would skim through it and miss key points of Rob and Lacey's vision.

And at the time, their Executive Summary section was *not* telling the right story.

Can you remember a time when you knew that getting something wrong would impact someone in a bad way? A time when your decision would impact someone else directly? When the pressure was on to get things perfect? That's how I felt with Lacey and Rob and their dream for The Vine House.

They were waiting for me to do things the right way; otherwise, they'd get blasted with an icy-cold, dream-shattering loan rejection. And I didn't want to let them down. I didn't want to be the reason they wouldn't get the funds they deserved, especially since they had sacrificed so much to get to that point.

The Executive Summary section was the absolute hardest part of working their business plan. Their draft touched the main points—the industry, the opportunity, the overview—but it didn't sell the story. It didn't boldly ask for the money needed or clearly show the perfection of their location.

Let Me Be Honest with You

Creating an Executive Summary incorrectly is like trying to get someone to pay full price for a house that is old, run-down, smelly, dirty, and filled with hideous furniture. That house may be sturdy and highly desirable, but it needs to be cleaned and staged before someone will be able to see its true potential. Your Executive Summary has the same need. It has to be a simple, clean, clutter-free piece of your business plan so the reader clearly understands the business potential at first glance.

In the end, I finished Rob and Lacey's Executive Summary with a specific structure and a simplified layout. I morphed their original summary in a way that kept it to one page while highlighting the most critical business facts. Lacey's words when she saw the first page were validation that I took the right approach: "Oh yes, *that's* what I'm talking about!"

Now the biggest question of all: Would it pass the final test? Would it get through underwriting? Would it get them the funding they needed?

The Goal of Your Executive Summary

The Executive Summary is supposed to be a place of focus. For this reason, I reject the notion that it should be written last. Instead, I encourage you to make this your first priority. I will walk you through what things to focus on, which will help you hone in on what matters most for the next steps of your business.

I had trouble with this section for The Vine House business plan because there was so much information and great elements I wanted to include. It was frustrating when I knew I had to choose one critical element over another. This Executive Summary chapter is meant to keep you focused on that goal. It's supposed to be challenging and a little uncomfortable, especially if there's a lot of greatness in your business vision.

Impact of This Section for Investors

The Executive Summary should be usable as a one- or two-page business plan or elevator pitch. It will be a test for investors, showing whether you understand your business and space well enough to clearly explain its nuances. It will also serve as their "first date" with your business idea. Do they feel a connection to your vision? Are they intrigued? Do they want to know more? These are the silent questions investors will ask as they review your Executive Summary.

Impact of This Section for Bankers

Business bankers and underwriters will look for facts in your Executive Summary. They already plan to read the rest of your business plan, but they know that this summary section will be the easiest and quickest way to interpret it. They will tend to search for the fundamentals of your business right here before diving into the pages of the rest of your plan. Missing details or critical components may frustrate them, especially if they have to hunt for simple answers in the rest of your business plan.

For Rob and Lacey's business plan, getting those key facts up front was a key goal. Their new business plan needed a few key elements, including a peek at the opportunity they were seizing and a clear industry descriptor. That would tell the underwriters what the business did and would offer a glimpse at the business potential. Those things would offer context right away and help the underwriters comfortably move on to read the full business plan.

Impact of This Section for Strategy

Having a narrowed focus is the ultimate goal for any business. If you are building your business plan to clarify your own strategy, this will help guide you to find a few specific answers. Can you clearly describe what space you are in, what customer niche you serve, and what value you are providing to the market? Are you able to add your revenue targets, any fund-raising needs, and what you plan to do in the next phase of your business? If not, that's okay. Any blanks you need to leave in the Executive Summary will be fillable later as you work through these open questions in the rest of your business plan.

The Executive Summary serves as that forcing function to make you focus and document your goals. If you can keep it to one page, it can be a great excerpt to print and post somewhere visible. That is especially helpful if you have a team or partner. Having this shared vision and intent for the business in a space where you are forced to be reminded of it every day will help you stay laser-focused on your goals for the business.

Creating Your Executive Summary

The Executive Summary is what will make your investor or lender have a solid (perhaps subconscious in some cases) opinion about your entire business, positive or negative. Many swear by the Executive Summary as the gateway section. If it is well written and includes the right details, the investor or lender is glad to read on, calmly and with an open mind.

However, if this section is not well assembled, then the reader can become instantly frustrated. He or she may start flipping through the business plan frantically in an irritated fashion. Your audience can be easily transformed into a hunting predator, searching aggressively in an attempt to find numbers, data, or strategic points of interest.

The Executive Summary is meant to be laser-tuned to your ultimate goal and mission. It should only include the core fundamentals of what you plan to do and how that paints a big picture. Too many little-picture details that are distracting or unhelpful can tend to be overwhelming.

Parts of an Executive Summary

This chapter reviews how to develop an Executive Summary with a specific format. With this format, you should have three core overview topics and a sidebar with additional details such as asking amount and year established.

Executive Summary

Industry

Asking Amount

Equity

Year Established

Market Need

Operating Status

Industry

Niche

Plan and Capital

Ideal Customer Persona

PROJECTIONS	YEAR 1	YEAR 2	YEAR 3
REVENUES			
COSTS			

If you are submitting your business plan to an investor, banker, or partner, know that their time is limited. In order to work within a simple framework and stay focused, consider the 3 x 3 rule. It will be useful in knowing when to stop writing so you don't end up with too much information crammed into your Executive Summary. Then, you can also consider adding an informational sidebar. I'll show you both of these elements now, starting with the 3 x 3 rule and following it with a design for your sidebar.

Part 1: The 3 x 3 Rule

Your Executive Summary is simply a one- or two-page pitch that tells a bit about your business and a bit about your goals. To make sure you stick to the points, you should only target three areas from a standard business plan table of contents and write three sentences in each area. For example, you can pick from the following:

Industry
Operations
Team
Customers
Market Need
Plan and Capital

The reason for choosing only three topics and three sentences for each is that it forces you to focus only on what is absolutely necessary and related to your business. That will help you avoid getting carried away with details. It will also leave room for you to add more critical information about your business. If absolutely needed, you can go to a five-sentence paragraph, but three is definitely the target.

For example, one of your paragraphs can be titled "Team." This is a great section to use as your first paragraph. I like to frame the first sentence this way: "Pajama Business LLC is operated by Mike Smith and Mary Jones." Don't list the whole organizational chart here; just let your audience know who the true "bosses" are in the business.

With Lacey and Rob, this was easy. They were the clear founders of the business. If you have more than two to three founders, however, you can list just the largest equity holder and then list the rest of the founders in your sidebar.

Another of your paragraphs can be titled "Industry." In the Industry paragraph, you can share three sentences about the problem in your industry that your business will solve. You should include whether your business is offering a complementary product or service to the industry or a brand new offering. Then state the size of the industry in which you will participate.

Your third paragraph is a great place to explain your need for funding. A subtitle such as "Plan and Capital" can introduce this section clearly. Here, you reiterate how much money you need, how you will use it, and what it will do for your business. Whether you need funds to buy land and build a new store, launch a six-figure marketing campaign, or just cover inventory costs for a few months, be sure to keep it simple and short. Here is an example of this paragraph:

> *The business requires $250,000 to launch. Funds will be used to secure a storefront, order initial equipment and furniture, and support the first three months of operation. This will allow the business to open with enough contingency funds to support unforeseen issues during the grand open.*

Once your core message is drafted in a few paragraphs, you can include a few extra details. The next points are critical if you are showing your plan to an investor, partner, or banker. They are most easily read as a sidebar on an Executive Summary page.

Part 2: Sidebar Details

Now that the core components of your Executive Summary are drafted in paragraph form, you need to add a few more details. Again, a sidebar format is simplest to create and easiest to read. The details included will help make sure the main factors of your business are readable in about 30 seconds.

"Slow readers can read 150–200 words in a minute – that drops to 50–75 words if the content is technical."*

These do not require paragraph-form writing, and you can add them as bullets or list them in abbreviated form. First, I'll tell you what goes into each piece; then, I'll share an example of a finished version.

Asking Amount

The first point is to state how much money you need. Even if you are building a business plan purely for strategy, this should be listed front and center as funds you plan to devote to the business from your savings or elsewhere.

If you are pitching to an investor or are pursuing a loan, there are a couple more points to mention. In your sidebar, add how much percentage of equity you intend to offer for an investor to consider. For a bank loan, list what interest rate percentage you are assuming.

Equity

In your sidebar, you also want to announce whether you have already distributed any equity. Stating any equity you have given away is a way of being transparent to your reader. It may also force you to come to terms with who has equity in your business and whether those people may need to be removed if their equity portion does not equal value brought to the business.

If you have more than two or three founders in your business, you can list the main one in the opening line of your Executive Summary, as described in

Note that some investors do not want to see several existing investors or equity distributions in the business. Be careful to only distribute equity to those who will bring long-term value to the company.

---

* (https://www.healthguidance.org/entry/13263/1/what-is-the-average-reading-speed-and-the-best-rate-of-reading.html)

"Part 1: The 3 x 3 Rule." Any founders not listed in that opening line should go in this Equity section of your sidebar. List their names and percent of equity they hold (e.g., Rob Britton – 50%).

Year Established

The third category is the year the business was established. There are several ways to approach this, including the following:

- List the date you set up your LLC or entity.
- List the year you started getting sales.
- List the current year as the year established if you are pre-sale and pre-entity.

Operating Status

List your operating status by showing whether your business is pre- or post-revenue. If you have sales, you are post-revenue. If you have never sold anything under the business name, you are pre-revenue.

Industry and Niche

The next part includes your industry and your niche in one to two words. Go broad for the industry; get more specific for the niche. For example, a set of pajamas would be in the clothing industry, and it would be niched in loungewear.

For Rob and Lacey, their industry was hospitality, and their niche was bed and breakfast in wine country.

Ironically, a bed and breakfast wasn't Rob and Lacey's original plan. In the early days, they envisioned opening a simple wedding venue. It's common for core components of a business vision to change, especially as you learn more about the business you are trying to start.

Ideal Customer Persona

Finally, describe your core customer. Is it a minor who attends school online from home and wants an everyday pajama set to wear? Is it a 45- to 55-year-old mother and wife who needs comfortable but presentable pajamas because her teenagers bring over friends unexpectedly? Is it a Millenial-aged professional who works from a home office three days a week? Allow yourself to describe your target audience in a few points.

In the end, your Executive Summary details may look like this:

Asking Amount: $135,000
Equity:
John Smith – 49%
Jane Smith – 49%
Early investor – 2%
Year Established: 2018
Operating Status: Pre-revenue
Industry: Clothing and Apparel
Niche: Loungewear
Ideal Customer Persona: Working professional who telecommutes and works from a home office

Remember, you need to be bold and clear. When you use the template provided with this book, you'll already be using a very simple and bold format. If you create your own document, remember that it should be scannable, have minimal text, and have snapshots of key information.

Also remember that laser focus is key. If you have multiple businesses or suboperations, you really need to stay singular with your message in the Executive Summary. Do not mention every direction your business could go or try to state every aspect of your business. Keep it high-level and simple, and do not overcomplicate your pitch.

Your target length should be about 500 words for the main paragraphs and about 50 words for the extra details. This is *not* a lot of text, and some people wonder how in the world they can get their whole business idea into so few words. Trust me, not only can you do it, but you'll be shocked at how much clearer your own vision is once you force yourself to cut extra explanation.

Things to Avoid

Avoid going beyond two pages. If you can, keep it to one page; that's ideal. Especially when pitching to investors and lenders, your goal is to make the reader feel informed yet compelled to read on. This strategy helps you avoid becoming overwhelmed while writing your Executive Summary and keeps your audience from being overwhelmed while reading it.

In your short Executive Summary, there is also specific language you want to avoid if you plan to send your business plan to an investor or a bank lender.

First, do not say, "If we only secure 1 percent of the industry, we'll make XX dollars" unless you have a clear, data-driven marketing strategy to get to this goal. Otherwise, this language is a sign that you do not have an acquisition strategy or a marketing plan, and it tells investors and lenders that you believe that just putting your product or service out there will result in customers. This is a common novice mistake.

Next, do not include "there's a million ways we could…" for how you will launch, market, sell, operate, and so on. Such a statement will not show that you are full of ideas. Instead, it will read like you are unfocused and have an unclear strategy. Try to avoid mentioning alternate strategies such as expanding beyond pajamas and into slippers and blankets. That can be introduced as a possibility later, in the Market Entry or Operations sections, but it does not belong in your Executive Summary.

Finally, if you are showing your Executive Summary to an investor or lender, be sure to stay in an educational mindset. Try not to "sell" just yet. For now, you are educating the investor or lender about this opportunity. Remember, you are introducing, not closing a deal. Stay brief and draw in your reader to want more detail. Stay high-level in your Executive Summary and lead with intrigue.

Technical Layout

There is a lot of detail to cram into the Technical Layout section. One way I format this section in my own business plan is with a core body of text, a text box with sidebar details, and a table with revenue projections.

When possible, try to add a picture. You can show your product, your ideal customer, or an image of something related to your business. If space is an issue and fitting an image isn't practical, it is okay to leave

Executive Summary — Pajama Business LLC

Pajama Business LLC is operated by Mike Smith and Mary Jones. It is a new business in Jacksonville, Florida, that offers comfortable pajamas that look like fashionable daywear. The business has a patent pending on the material for its main product line.

Seeking $135,000

John Smith – 49%
Jane Smith – 49%
Early investor – 2%

Industry

Pajama Business LLC will operate within an $8 billion dollar industry. Within this industry, sleepwear is lumped with lingerie, and the market is shifting to segment sleepwear apart from intimates. The business owners see opportunity to start operating within the space with a revolutionary new material. Currently, there are three direct competitors identified in this area who will be challenged by our business on quality and atmosphere.

2018

Pre-revenue

Market Need

Clothing and Apparel

Pajama Business LLC targets audiences at home who are looking to be comfortable but presentable at all times. This includes individuals who work from a home office, individuals living with roommates or large families, and others. Most options available are uncomfortable, too casual, or lack versatility. Our product is breathable, customizable, and suited for wear inside and even outside of the home.

Loungewear / Sleepwear

Working professional who telecommutes and works from a home office

Plan and Capital

The business requires $135,000 to launch. Funds will be used to secure a storefront, order initial equipment and furniture, and support the first three months of operation. This will allow the business to open with enough contingency funds to support unforeseen issues during the grand opening.

Ideal customers will wear our pajamas while working from home.

PROJECTIONS	YEAR 1	YEAR 2	YEAR 3
REVENUES	$155,000	$275,000	$390,000
COSTS	$149,000	$135,000	$125,000

it out. However, if you do include a picture, be sure to put a caption beneath it that explains why you included it or what the picture shows.

Adding a table that lists revenues and costs is a simple way to introduce the size of your company without becoming burdened by the financials too early in the business plan.

Since your financials may be completed last, simply add a placeholder for now, and you can fill in the numbers later.

Usually, having revenue projections in the Executive Summary is essential. It shows growth potential and brings immediate clarity to the size of the business. However, having numbers that don't grow much year-over-year or numbers that are low compared to the amount of funding you are requesting can reflect negatively if they are taken out of context of the full financials.

If your revenues in the first three years don't move upward by at least 5 percent year-over-year, then you might omit the revenue table in this section and encourage your reader to review your financials in the context of your cash flows, balance sheets, and income statements later in the business plan.

Finishing The Vine House Business Plan

When I built the Executive Summary section for Rob and Lacey, I had to make a tough decision. This was a rare case where I didn't opt to show the financial projections in the Executive Summary. Their projections were realistic and conservative and showed healthy year-over-year growth, but there was a need to explain the opportunity more fully.

Executive Summary

The Vine House B&B is a family-established business in Temecula, California, that offers lodging in the wine country region. The business is owned by Lacey and Robert Britton, who live on site. With three years experience running a five-star Airbnb vacation rental unit on the current property, the owners are preparing for the next phase of business expansion by converting their two-story barn into a seven-unit bed and breakfast.

Industry

The business has acquired property located directly on the De Portola Wine Trail, surrounded by wineries and wedding venues. Large-scale winery-owned lodging in neighboring vicinities are not equipped to provide customers with the same intimate experience as a bed and breakfast, as lodging is seen as an ancillary service to the primary business of wine sales. At the Vine House hospitality *is* our business!

Opportunity

The De Portola Wine Trail does not have a single lodging facility despite heavy tourist activity. The Vine House B&B will be the first and only lodging option on the wine trail. Preliminary referral and discount arrangements have been discussed with several surrounding wineries and wedding venues. The business will work particularly closely with neighboring winery Oak Mountain, providing direct access to wedding room blocks and room discounts for wine club members; wine tasting discounts at Oak Mountain will be offered to guests of the Vine House.

The Ask:
Seeking $1,075,000

The Need:
Capital will be used to fund CapEx and OpEx associated with launching a new bed and breakfast

Equity:
Robert & Lacey Britton
90% Owners
Mary Britton (Robert's mother)
10% owner

Location:
Temecula, California

Industry:
Hospitality

Niche:
Bed and breakfast in Wine Country

Customers:
Tourists and wedding parties

Had I been building this for an investor instead of a loan underwriter, I would have opted to keep the revenue table. However, knowing the loan team would absolutely get to the financials as part of their review process, I opted to use the extra page space to explain some of the arrangements and agreements that Lacey and Rob were already putting into motion for The Vine House.

They were creating a network—well ahead of business open—that would create the circumstances needed to succeed. Their business exists in an area where they will capture an entire mini-market on the De Portola Wine Trail, a highly traveled tourist area that regularly hosts weddings and events. This area is well connected, and the businesses support one another in this tight-knit community. Rob and Lacey had already begun creating relationships within that exclusive group, knowing that they would need local allies to truly see business success. Their networking was already paying off, and they secured verbal agreements for mutual client referrals well before the business even formally existed. This fact belonged in the Executive Summary.

In the end, the business plan was accepted by the underwriters, and Lacey and Rob received the loan they needed to launch The Vine House. They did it despite tons of hurdles and unexpected turns with the land, design, and build plans. They did it over the course of a few years while juggling a growing family.

The passion Rob and Lacey had when I worked with them was tangible. Getting a glimpse of what they went through behind the scenes was amazing, and I am still shocked at the ups and downs they experienced while launching their business. What stood out the most, though, was their energy. It was always positive, customer-focused, and absolutely contagious. It made me wonder how two people could do this all on their own and still find the energy to encourage one another.

Don't Get Stuck: How to Get Started

To start your Executive Summary, plug in the easy answers for now. You may not have all the details quite yet, but that's okay. Some of the answers will appear and even change as you work through the rest of your business plan sections.

As soon as you finish entering these early details of your Executive Summary, you can move on to a section where you *will* know all the answers. That section is the Executive Team section. The next chapter will review what to include and how to position yourself and any other founders of the business.

My Executive Summary includes:

❑　My 3x3 points

❑　My sidebar details

❑　My revenue table

Chapter 2

Executive Team

*This is the area where you learn the most. I spend time with my wife and children, but then I'm with my partner **all day**. It's crucial to have the right co-founder to do this with. The team dynamic is so critical.*

—Billy Rinchin, co-founder of Kimove

www.kimove.com

Kimove

I'll never forget how overwhelmed I felt when I worked with Billy Rinchin, co-founder of Kimove, on his business plan. He was working on his first invention, which has since inspired the team to create a totally different business that leverages the same technology. At the time, when they were working on their original business concept before Kimove, the team needed outside capital to move that business forward. So, Billy was working on the launch of a crowdfunding campaign.

The technology that Billy and his team created allows a handheld device to sense your movements and translate them to a digital device such as a smartphone. Originally, there was a vision to use those movements to correlate with electronic sound so that users could create music with a simple gesture or wave of their hand. Even though the business has changed how it plans to use the technology, the device remains an augmented reality product. Its new purpose is to promote healthy screen-time for children ages two through eight. It combines the movement-sensing technology the team developed with customized shows and interactive content to encourage kids to physically and vocally engage with what they are watching. Simply put, it addresses the couch-potato problem associated with excessive screen time and encourages kids to get moving.

When I was working with Billy on his original invention, he had been told by the crowdfunding folks that he needed to have a business plan developed in a very specific way. He needed demographic, psychographic, and sociographic profiling of his target audience completed before they would launch his campaign. When Billy contacted me, it was a matter of seconds before I heard the voice of one of his team members on the other end of the line. Together, they expressed their situation and the blood, sweat, and tears they had poured into the business thus far. I immediately felt empathy for their journey. On another phone call, more team members were on the other end of the line. During that second call, while I was intrigued at how involved the team members seemed to be in this early phase, I had another train of thought running. I was panicking about whether I could take this project.

The overwhelming panic I felt was related to the timing of the whole thing. I recognized right away that this would be a more intense business plan than the others, and I was already scheduled to travel for conferences. I thought about turning Billy and his team away, but I knew they were on a specific deadline for launching this campaign. They needed this done ASAP. Besides, this kind of project needed a specific approach, and I wasn't sure that the other provider I would refer them to would be able to support this with the right level of quality.

It was in this moment that I wished I had my own team like Billy did, someone else to help me and share the workload. Can you remember a time when you felt like you had too many top-priority things to do? Worse, you felt like those things could only be done by you and no one else. That's exactly the weight I was feeling in that moment.

I accepted Billy as a client. While that business plan was extremely difficult because of the timing, it was even more of a challenge because of the scope. A hefty amount of market research and analysis was needed for the plan, and I carefully planned windows of work time to get it all finished. I sat in airports and hotel rooms, pecking away at the details of the document whenever I had a spare minute between seminars and conference events. I seemed to get a slew of calls during those two weeks, and they were from clients who needed a business plan done *now*. I wanted so badly to take those projects, but I simply didn't have the bandwidth. It tangibly hurt me to turn them away and refer them to other providers whom I knew could offer immediate solutions, albeit for higher prices.

The absolute biggest struggle with Billy's plan was getting the Executive Team section just right. The team was huge compared to most founding teams. I first approached it with a hacksaw, thinking everyone listed could not possibly belong on the core founders list. However, after reviewing the role of each member, I reluctantly admitted that each person belonged in the Executive Team section. Now the question was, how would I add them all in a way that wouldn't destroy the flow of the section?

Let Me Be Honest with You

Putting too many people in the founding section is like trying to shove 72 crayons into a 68-count box. It's going to look bloated, messy, and entirely distracting. I was trying to avoid that with Billy and his team.

In the end, the plan was finished on time, with the longest list of Executive Team members I had included to date. It took some creativity to make sure every member had a proper background without cluttering up the section. I used a layout and text rhythm that allowed everyone to fit nicely. Billy sent it right over to his crowdfunding folks for their use in his campaign.

The Goal of Your Executive Team Section

The Executive Team section will show the founders of the business. This is not the place to list the full organizational team. That will come later. Here, only list the individuals who are launching or creating the business.

Had I been building Billy's business plan for capital investors or bankers, I would have approached his Executive Team section a bit differently. It would have been capped at two executive decision-makers and would have talked a bit more about each member's character and ability to lead, in addition to listing their experience. Instead, as you'll see in a few pages, I opted for brevity on each team member and only covered the basics. That sufficed for Billy's situation.

Impact of This Section for Investors

Investors will review this section to gauge the founder(s). Background, motive, and indicators of personality will be considered as an investor reviews the owner's biography. In essence, the investor wants to know the answers for two burning questions: Does this person/team have what it takes to succeed? Can I work with this person/team in partnership long term?

Giving an investor more than two partners to think about can lead to confusion. Limit this to the true decision-makers in your business. That way, your investor can focus on equal counterparts within the founding team.

Impact of This Section for Bank Loan Applications

Loan underwriters will review this section to understand what is at stake for the founder(s) in starting this business. The bank wants to know that you will do anything and everything needed to make the business succeed, which usually requires motives beyond repaying the loan. Underwriters will wonder: Is anyone dependent on the founder(s) financially? Does the founder have a track record of playing things safe?

Listing more than two founders can complicate things in under-writing. Whenever possible, the Executive Team section for an under-writer review should be hyper-focused on the loan applicants. This keeps the underwriting review simple.

Impact of This Section for Strategy

This section is your *why*. It requires you to face yourself and get honest about how you may or may not be ready to create this business. Entrepreneurs can forget that there's an extremely irrational component to starting a business. In this section, you have to face that irrationality. You have to answer these questions: Am I doing this for the right reasons? Am I over-playing or underestimating where I will bring real value in this business?

When I talked with Billy about his *why*, we covered some raw drivers behind his ambitions. Originally, starting down his entrepreneurial path was full of romanticizing the road ahead. He was willing to move his family from Mongolia to California to make his business dreams a reality. He admits that he didn't have a ton of knowledge in business and was learning along the way. He described launching a business like shooting for Mars. He knew his original vision could be described as far-fetched, but he felt it was worth it to start down this path. Success could mean changing his own life, the lives of his family members, and the lives of each team member who dedicated their time and energy to this project. We wanted to reach Mars for all of them, and that drove him forward. He couldn't let them down.

Working this section into your business plan early helps you answer why for yourself before pouring everything you have into this business idea. Be honest with yourself as you work through it. If you find that your *why* isn't strong enough, if the irrationality of starting this business refuses to go away, then maybe you need to reevaluate. That doesn't mean that you abandon your business idea, but maybe pivoting to something that aligns with your core values and beliefs can be worked into your business concept.

The following will review the core components your Executive Team section should cover. It will examine the high-level topics to consider. It will also offer sample details you can consider as you write the Executive Team section of your business plan.

Creating Your Executive Team Section

There are several parts you can include in your Executive Team section. This section serves as a short biography of the founders. The biography should include every major accomplishment you have made that leads to why you are now ready to run a business. This section will review the following six topics you need to cover in order to complete this section correctly:

- Education
- Years of professional experience
- Awards and accomplishments
- Previous experience in entrepreneurship
- Baseline character traits
- A headshot

First, let's review how to incorporate your education into your Executive Summary.

Education

Your educational achievements should consist of the basics. If you have any degrees, go ahead and list them, along with the name of the school. Aside from graduating with honors or other notable achievements, try to avoid an abundance of detail such as GPA or specific classes you have taken. You want to keep this as brief and high-level as possible and avoid approaching it like a résumé or job application.

In this section, avoid listing dates, if possible. Ageism is a real bias, and you can bet people will try to reverse-engineer how old you are based on when you went to college and such. Just leave dates out of it! Instead of trying to calculate your age, they will simply revert to trying to guess whether you are experienced or not, which is all they should care about anyway.

If you do not have a formal education that you feel comfortable listing, that's okay. You can start with the Professional Experience section first if that is the case.

Professional Experience

The Professional Experience section is where you can showcase any background you have as a worker or employee. You should include a sentence or two summarizing where you have worked and what roles you have played. Any work experience that may have brought you to where you are or that contributes to your ability to be a great business leader should be included. Next, you will write about any awards and accomplishments you earned from employers, certifying institutions, or schools.

Awards and Accomplishments

The Awards and Accomplishments section can—and should—be a showcase of your achievements. Anything related to professional certificates, school awards, public service, and organizational recognition should be listed here. Also consider accomplishments related to volunteer projects and community efforts. These are great character points, and including them helps paint a holistic picture. To round out your experience, the next section will focus on your experience in entrepreneurship.

Veteran designation or government service experience should be listed in this section as well.

Experience in Entrepreneurship

Your experience in even the simplest of business types brings huge value to your business plan. Remember that lemonade stand you started at age eight? Things like that count in your favor! It shows a trend. It implies you have entrepreneurial blood in your veins. Think hard about what you have ever dabbled in, whether it was a formal business or not. A hobbyist photographer who sells prints online is an entrepreneur. A school teacher who does tutoring in the summer months is an

Remember: Experience starting or running a business of any kind is always your most important thing to highlight, even more than education or awards. And, of course, include failures, too. Failed businesses are still started businesses, so write about them as a growth experience. Try not to get hung up on any business closures or having a business that ended.

entrepreneur. Think about any endeavor in which you were responsible for selling a product or service or where profit or loss was 100 percent your responsibility to manage. These things count as experience, no matter how informal.

Baseline Character Traits

Now that you've expressed your background and experience, you should share some intangible pieces of information about your character. Describing your best character traits can feel awkward, but this is an area where you need to brag about yourself in a very careful way. Here, your intent is to show that you have the fundamental pillars of leadership.

To show this, include baseline character traits in your language. For instance:

> *Others describe Billy as a natural leader. No matter the circumstance, people tend to gravitate to Billy's collaborative management style and ability to see things objectively.*

Other great words include the following:

Dedicated
Reliable
Determined
Open-minded

These words show your best features as an entrepreneur. If you feel self-conscious about bragging, ask someone close to you for 10 words they would use to describe you, and run with those. Now is not the time to be modest or feel shy. Get bold and be proud of who you are! It will clearly shine through your words when writing.

Now that you've expressed the best parts of your background and character, you can move on to show yourself fully in your business plan with a headshot.

Headshot

A headshot is simply a picture of you from the chest up. Your picture should be in your business plan biography. Period. Many entrepreneurs feel exposed when doing this. Some are afraid to be judged on their appearance. It is common to have a specific fear of bias. People are afraid to be judged by things such as race, weight, attractiveness, gender, and so on. Some new entrepreneurs are even afraid of failure and of associating their identities with a business that may not survive the volatile first years.

Billy and his team experienced racism, bias, and other discrimination is-sues while hunting for investors, even with firms that specialized in mi-nority and immigrant financing. However, there are also lots of investors who are seeking diversity, so be careful not to let a negative experience discourage you.

While all of these fears are legitimate and understandable, there is more value to be gained than lost. Showing your face is important. Having a smiling image of yourself in your business plan can impact the way you will be seen. You want to show yourself as a trustworthy entrepreneur. While it may seem a bit superficial, there is plenty of sci-ence to prove that human brains are quick to pass judgment on a per-son based on their facial expression in a photo. In 2008, two Princeton University scientists, Nikolaas N. Oosterhof and Alexander Todorov, conducted experiments that proved that humans make grand inferences about a person based on facial expression.[1] Their research proved what humankind has assumed for centuries, that we are highly prone to make quick judgments based on a face. Even the most objective individuals are naturally prone to this. It is simply the way our brains are wired, so it shouldn't be viewed as a good or bad thing. It is simply a reality in the way our minds work.[2]

Now, in order for your image in your business plan to work in your favor, you need to do more than paste a dry, unsmiling snapshot of yourself. Often when I ask for a picture from clients, they return with a quick, somewhat awkward selfie, usually not smiling. Or, if they are smiling, it is in a really shy way that comes across as unconfident. That kind of image can actually hurt your business plan if you intend to show it to investors, partners, or bank underwriters. Your smiling, happy face will help trigger positive perceptions in your audience.

It sounds a bit dramatic, but simply thinking of something that genuinely makes you feel joy right before snapping that picture will make a world of difference!

A positive perception is especially important for a possible partner, evaluating underwriter, or future investor. That person wants to know who they are dealing with, and adding a human element to the business plan creates *instant* connection. By seeing your image, they will already start to develop a personal feel for you even before they have met you to talk about details.

Besides, they will look you up online anyway, so which is a better first impression: a polished image you add to your plan or a random Facebook image they find on their own?

---

1. N.N. Oosterhof and A. Todorov, "The Functional Basis of Face Evaluation," *Proceedings of the National Academy of Sciences* 105, no. 32 (2008): 11087–11092, https://psych.princeton.edu/file/167/download?token=4dQtqVRf.
2. Leslie A. Zebrowitz and Joann M. Montepare, "Social Psychological Face Perception: Why Appearance Matters," *Social and Personality Psychology Compass* 2.3 (2008): 1497, https://www.ncbi.nlm.nih.gov/pmc/articles/PMC2811283/.

For your headshot, consider these tips and nuances to consider as you snap the photo.

Headshot Tips and Nuances

To make taking your headshot more comfortable, try the following:

- Invest 10 minutes in putting on a nice shirt and making sure your hair is presentable.
- Have someone take a picture of you in a place where there is a lot of natural light (a cell phone camera is fine).
- The shot should be your head and shoulders with a cut-off just below your collarbone.
- Avoid covering up your neck; neck exposure reveals that you are trustworthy and honest. It also sends a message that you hold your head high and are confident.

Things to Avoid

There are a few things to be careful of when writing your Executive Team section. While you want to mention your personal motivators, try to avoid getting overly specific about your family life. Again, subconscious bias can creep in as people try to gauge whether you will have time to run a business when you are a parent of four kids, have a ton of personal hobbies, or are actively in the dating scene.

Also, avoid personal hobbies you cannot tout as being helpful in your business knowledge. Talk about hobbies as they relate to your entrepreneurial journey, and stop there. For instance, revealing that you spend every weekend practicing your golf swing may not be valuable to your business plan unless it relates to your intentions to run your own driving range.

When the investor or business banker reads your business plan and likes the business concept, you can get chummy later and talk personal and recreational stuff, but it should be all business for now. The furthest you should go with personal details is stating you are a mother or father, a husband or wife, but try to avoid mentioning how old your kids are or how long you have been married. I have seen firsthand how one investor can interpret this differently from another. Some investors are more self-aware than most and work to not pass judgment in these areas. Others are the opposite and believe they can make huge inferences about people based on minimal information. The latter group is who you are protecting yourself from.

Finally, avoid listing the details of your background in bullets or list layout. This is a narrative and should be in story format. Talk about what you have done, perhaps mention when you had the pivot point for starting your business, and mention your character traits as a last sentence or paragraph. Overall, your mini-biography should be rather short and can run from a few paragraphs to as brief as one paragraph.

Technical Layout

Most business plan templates and guides lump the Executive Team together with the Operations Team. The instructions in these templates ask that you include each executive member's operational role and responsibilities. This is somewhat subjective, and I'm sharing what has worked best for my clients based on format testing with investors.

The grand conclusion: There seems to be a better response with first stating *what* is the idea followed by *who* is behind the idea. That is why I recommend following your Executive Summary section with your Executive Team section. Focusing on the founder in a personable way in the Executive Team section also leaves room to focus on the roles and duties of that person later in the business plan, in the Operations section. That allows readers to feel a connection with the founder behind the business without diving into the technical aspects of the business too early in the plan.

If your business has one person at the main helm, then your Executive Team chapter will be one page maximum with a great headshot of the founder. If you like, you can also use subheadings to break up each section, such as Professional Experience and Accomplishments.

Executive Team Overview

Pajama Business LLC

Johnny Smith, CEO

Johnny Smith, the original founder, has more than 20 years experience in concrete-pouring projects on the Lakeshore Drive thruway. His progressive history as a union worker allowed him to work as foreman and superintendent on various noteworthy projects. From his reputation as a hard worker with a high-quality perspective to his clear leadership style and unprecedented levels of integrity, he is a top choice for many notorious hotels in the area.

Johnny is motivated to succeed in this business. Being an entrepreneur was a childhood dream, and he has full support and encouragement from his wife and children. Professionally, Johnny is well known for being someone who motivates workers on any project. He is fair and has admirable character. With a keen ability to see the big picture without missing the important details, he is hired when business owners expect high exposure on their projects. His say-do ratio for keeping budget and schedule are well above average compared to others in the industry, again attesting to his integrity.

Johnny's projects have won multiple awards throughout his career for skill and workmanship, including one from the Concrete Institute for the Best Concrete Project. Such awards bring benefits and revenue-generating attention to the business owners which makes him a favored contractor in the area. Johnny will bring his talents to benefit the long-term success of Concrete Business LLC through clear management and strategic alignment to key projects.

Johnny Smith, CEO

Graduated *Summa Cum Laude* with honors from Phoenix University

Active contracts License Exp. 11/22

Finishing Billy's Business Plan

When I built the Executive Team section for Billy's original invention, there were two problems. The first was the length of the section. There were eight founders to list, and I knew the section couldn't exceed two pages. Any longer than that would lose the reader. Normally, a proper founder list has a half page per founder or one full page if there is only one founder.

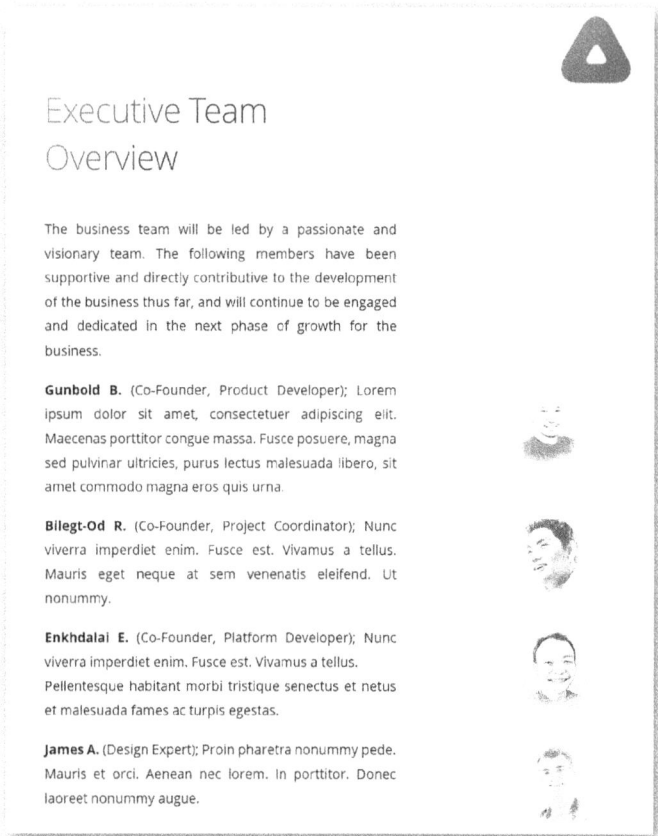

Executive Team Overview

The business team will be led by a passionate and visionary team. The following members have been supportive and directly contributive to the development of the business thus far, and will continue to be engaged and dedicated in the next phase of growth for the business.

Gunbold B. (Co-Founder, Product Developer); Lorem ipsum dolor sit amet, consectetuer adipiscing elit. Maecenas porttitor congue massa. Fusce posuere, magna sed pulvinar ultricies, purus lectus malesuada libero, sit amet commodo magna eros quis urna.

Bilegt-Od R. (Co-Founder, Project Coordinator); Nunc viverra imperdiet enim. Fusce est. Vivamus a tellus. Mauris eget neque at sem venenatis eleifend. Ut nonummy.

Enkhdalai E. (Co-Founder, Platform Developer); Nunc viverra imperdiet enim. Fusce est. Vivamus a tellus. Pellentesque habitant morbi tristique senectus et netus et malesuada fames ac turpis egestas.

James A. (Design Expert); Proin pharetra nonummy pede. Mauris et orci. Aenean nec lorem. In porttitor. Donec laoreet nonummy augue.

To work within a two-page limit, their business plan had a short overview of each member in order to fit four people per page. To combat the fact that each person only had a snippet of spotlight, I created a strong introductory paragraph to set the tone that each team member is a key person in the organization.

The second problem with writing their Executive Team section related to featuring founder photos. Multiple team members felt insecure about including their faces in the business plan. Some were afraid to be judged by their weight, and others were concerned about racial or ethnic bias. Billy was wise on this point, though. He knew that anyone who judged them based on appearance in the business plan would also judge them when they eventually met in person. Any investor with prejudice would be automatically filtered out at the business plan stage before time was wasted and hopes were high with a possible partnership.

One great workaround was showing each person in sketch art form. The idea came directly from the team, as they had used this headshot format in the past for other presentations. I plugged in these grayscale sketch images of each person, just clear enough to offer a human element but conservative enough to elicit comfort so no team member felt over-exposed. In the end, the two-page Executive Team section did the entire team justice.

Don't Get Stuck: How to Get Started

To get started on your Executive Team section, begin with your own background. If you are drawing a blank on where to focus, consider these prompts:

1. How long have you wanted to do this business venture?
2. Tell the story of the defining moment when this dream sparked in you. What led to this moment?
3. Why is this your dream (business, company, mission, etc.)?
4. Who are you passionate about helping with your idea and why (family member, partner, unique needs of customers)?

As you finish this section, you will be making a transition away from the story of you. You will spend the next chapters focusing on your business and the market in which it operates. In Chapter 3, you will dive into understanding your macro industry, the greater arena in which your business will participate.

My Executive Team Section includes:

- ❑ Founders' education
- ❑ Founders' professional experience
- ❑ Founders' awards and accomplishments
- ❑ Founders' experience in entrepreneurship
- ❑ Founders' baseline character traits
- ❑ Founders' headshot(s)

Chapter 3

Macro Industry

Research is a funny thing. Just as the word states, you have to "research" for information. As long as you have a phone, computer, iPad – then there's no lack of information out there.

—Milo Cavalcante, co-founder of Traffic SAMS™ Inc.

But you need to have data from a reliable source. The thing is, we can Google stuff all day, but if it's not coming from a good source, it's all useless.

—Omar Lynn, co-founder of Traffic SAMS™ Inc.

www.trafficsamsinc.com

Milo Cavalcante first contacted me to help with one of his business plans, and I felt excited because he said he had already done research that I could leverage. As an innovative entrepreneur, he and his partner Omar Lynn were working through a couple of different business launches. They had already successfully launched The Cue Mate, a patented product that is making a huge impact on the world of pool tables and billiard rooms. Meanwhile, they were also working to launch a business founded on a new innovation. The invention could truly disrupt the traffic safety industry.

Milo and Omar are a well balanced team. Milo's background and affinity for sales and Omar's experience and analytical nature make them a strong force together. They recognize the strength in each other and have a healthy respect for one another's areas of expertise. They met as colleagues and became business partners after unexpected layoffs. They turned a challenging time into a time of opportunity. When I'm in their presence, their positive energy is absolutely palpable.

One of their latest businesses, Traffic SAMS™, is built around a road safety sign invention. It is one that replaces large portable digital message boards attached to trailers that are often used in construction zones. Among several unique features, their sign is innovative in the way it connects to a safety barrel instead of a trailer, opening the doors to tons of potential applications. With smaller dimensions, lower cost, lighter weight, and quicker deployment than traditional alternatives, their invention would set a new standard in the market.

Milo and Omar were raising a few million dollars and had line of sight for the business to generate more than $300 million in revenues by year three. They had already gotten past the concept phase and drummed up serious interest in the New York area to launch their first product rollout. Now, a business plan was needed to impress the right audience. Hoping to pitch this to other businesses in the industry and to interested investors, they wanted to use this plan to secure the funding needed to take things to the next level.

When they first reached out to me, I had little knowledge of the variable message board market. I had no idea of the wide range of applications, the variety of market players, or the nuances of city contracts available for sign providers. So when they shared their market research information, I was elated to have a good starting point. But I soon realized that I still needed more information in order to finish the business plan.

Have you ever been in the middle of traffic and decided to try a new, different route? Maybe at first you were unsure of your decision, but soon you were flying down traffic-free streets, so grateful that you didn't have to sit in that bumper-to-bumper craziness. Then you arrive at your destination only to realize you didn't really save any time. You may have avoided traffic, but it wasn't much of a shortcut after all.

That's how I felt when I tackled this research. The existing material they had from a research provider was a great starting point, but there wasn't enough of the *right* information. It was a lot to sift through, and I spent a lot of time trying pull out useful pieces of content, which were few and far between.

To this day, I remember the greatest challenge I had was swimming through the research. There was just so much information out there. I wondered how I was supposed to capture everything needed without over-complicating this business plan for investors.

Let Me Be Honest with You

Less is more when it comes to the final research for your business plan. Have you ever picked up a huge book and thought, "Wow, I bet there's some great stuff in here," and then put it back on the shelf knowing you'll never read such a monstrous book? Have you ever started reading a news article and found yourself skimming past the fluff in search of the highlights? Maybe you have even moved to audio books and find yourself tuning out during certain parts, essentially skimming the content with your ears.

Heck, maybe you're even skimming through this book right now. That's okay, no judgment! That's just more proof of the point.

Investors, bankers, and partners will do the same thing with your business plan if it is too jam-packed with information. A lengthy research section will lull the human brain into skimming. If you keep your research section short, simple, and visual, you will increase the odds of your audience easily reading, interpreting, and understanding it. Treat it like a summary, not a complete encyclopedia of your industry.

By default, you will find a ton of information you can justify including in your business plan. However, if no one reads it, you are literally wasting time writing pages and pages of researched content. Your research needs to tell a simple story, a story that explains the big picture and then the smaller picture. You need to walk yourself and any future readers down a path that shows how your business will fit into the grand scheme of the business universe.

The Goal of Your Macro Industry Section

Your Macro Industry research section is meant to educate and inform you and your reader about the big picture for your business space. Most people spend precious hours on this section that they'll never get back. And all of those hours usually result in too much information that isn't relevant to their business in the end.

That is usually because of these silent questions:

How much information is enough?
How much should I research?
How many pages of data and statistics and trends should I include?
Should I copy and paste pieces of research reports?
What matters and what doesn't?

This chapter will give you the answers to these questions. Simplified into three basic steps, it will guide you to focus on what matters most and will help you include only the most necessary pieces of information.

Impact of This Section for Investors

The Macro Industry research section will be used as a baseline for investors to understand your industry. If you are pitching to investors who are not familiar with your space, they may see this as a mini-crash course in your industry. However, if they are familiar with your industry, they will look for how you interpret the space and the trends. That is why putting information into your own words is critical; they will see a copy-paste job from websites and research reports a mile away. That approach is considered lazy, and they will not appreciate that tactic.

For the business plan I worked on with Milo and Omar, developing research in a way that focused on the right macro industry was a challenge. The variable sign market is one that has both very clear niches and blurred lines among categories. It was critical to showcase the right pieces of the industry for investors, and unfortunately, I had a hard time finding one single report that completely showed the target space.

I want to help you avoid the pain I went through. That is why this Macro Industry chapter shows you how to gather information beyond what may be shown in a pre-canned report. Those reports are wonderful, but for some businesses, they simply don't cover the right areas, especially if you need to prepare your business plan for an investor to interpret.

Impact of This Section for Bankers

Business bankers and underwriters will look for trends of steadiness and stability in your Macro Industry section. They will be less likely to care about whether or not you borrowed all your data from a research report. However, they will want to see that your industry is low in volatility and rather predictable. For this reason, they will focus on how the industry has grown, shrunk, or pivoted in recent years. They will also look for what experts predict for industry growth in the future.

Impact of this Section for Strategy

The strategy in your business should be rooted in where the industry is headed and what it needs most. Taking this broader perspective can reveal greater trends you may not have been aware of prior to doing this research. That is why pulling from your own knowledge or approaching research with the intent of validating what you already know tends to be a bad idea.

Creating Your Macro Analysis

For most businesses, the research should be generally available. However, there may be some careful digging or even triangulating needed. That is why you need to understand this point before you start researching:

> If you feel like your business doesn't fit neatly within a specific industry, it's okay to pick another industry that is close to yours or is an umbrella that includes your industry.

For instance, if you are a contractor who specializes in laying tile flooring, you may not be able to find industry reports on your specific niche within a broader industry. Instead, you may need to look for industry reports on construction, which would include your business as a subindustry. Even though tile contractors would never call themselves general construction contractors, taking high-level growth trends from this sector can make sense as long as you state how those trends apply to or impact your specific subindustry.

How to Focus on the Right Data

The market research of a business plan is usually a stressful concept because you can end up researching about your industry for days. You may find conflicting information. You may find that most details are interesting, but you may be unsure about whether they belong in the business plan. You may have questions about how long your research section should be, what kinds of statistics to include, and whether you need charts, tables, or graphs.

Without these answers, entrepreneurs just keep going—researching and writing, researching and writing, for pages and pages.

Here is the good news: There is a way to simplify this section to a few key points. You will see that it really does not have to be a painfully intense exercise. For an effective Macro Industry research section, you only need to research a couple of specific questions.

Checkpoint: Remember Your References Page

First and foremost, get your References page or document component handy. You'll use it the most in this section and the next two sections of your business plan. On the References page, you will simply list what data you found and where you found it. That will be important for investors and bankers to prove that

References

Invacare. (2019). Product Catalog - Electric Beds. Retrieved from http://www.invacare.com/cgi-bin/imhqprd/inv_catalog/prod_cat_detail.jsp

Texas City, TX demographics. 2004. AreaVibes.com. Retrieved from https://www.areavibes.com/texas+city-tx/demographics/

you got the information from credible sources. For your own strategy purposes, it will be useful later when you need to go back and reference things you may come across in your research. To cite your references, note the name of the provider, the year the data was published, the title of the article, the page on which it appeared, and the URL where you found the fact or insight.

Now that your References page is handy, you can dive into the core of your research.

Conducting Macro Industry Research
Step 1: Find Your NAICS Code

In order to get started, you will need to know what the applicable NAICS code is for your business.

> The North American Industry Classification System (NAICS) is the standard used by Federal statistical agencies in classifying business establishments for the purpose of collecting, analyzing, and publishing statistical data related to the U.S. business economy.*

If you are unsure of what your NAICS code is, you can visit https://www.naics.com/search/ to find your code based on a keyword search. Finding your code will help you with the next steps in your research.

Conducting Macro Industry Research
Step 2: Clarify the Size and Projected Growth of the Industry

After you have your NAICS code, you can use it to find the size of your macro industry. This simply means researching the revenue dollars your

---

https://www.census.gov/eos/www/naics/.

industry creates or, in other words, how much money is made in that industry every year. Without an NAICS code, you can literally Google "size of car wash industry," "mobile app industry revenue," or "how big is the apparel industry." However, your results may be skewed or inflated without the narrowed specifics of your NAICS code.

With your NAICS code, you have the power to pull existing research reports for your macro industry, some free and some for a fee. For instance, you can buy a comprehensive report from a site such as www.IBISWorld.com. This is the solution I use; most professionals in my industry prefer IBISWorld. These reports tend to be well developed and easy to read and come with interpretations and analyses. That saves you time and brainpower.

Another solution you can try is the United States Census Bureau's Industry Statistics Portal at https://www.census.gov/econ/isp/. It has great information you can access for free, including visual charts, graphs, and tables that will look great in your business plan. Consider the United States Census Bureau for statistics that show growth or size of your industry, which will be classified and sortable by NAICS industry code. The data on this site is fantastic, although you should expect to spend some time viewing all the metrics and information. It will not come with interpretations like a formal report, but as a free resource, it is certainly useful, and the information you need is likely there.

As you look at data for your specific industry, pull out answers that address the growth projections for your macro industry. Depending on your source of information, you will look for phrases such as "growth **projection,**" "industry **trend,**" and "market **change.**"

Below are additional sites that are great for digging and researching more into your market:

- Federal Statistics – https://www.data.gov
- U.S. Government Open Data – https://www.usa.gov/business
- U.S. Department of Commerce – https://www.commerce.gov
- Bureau of Economic Analysis – https://www.bea.gov
- U.S. Small Business Administration – https://www.sba.gov/

- Bureau of Labor Statistics – https://www.bls.gov/
- Flodoggie – www.flodoggie.com

Here are some questions you will want to answer in your research:

- Is the industry growing or shrinking?
- Does the industry have a dominant company that owns a large percentage of the market?
- What is the segmentation of the market (e.g., 50% of the lingerie market is pajama wear sales)?
- How is the industry different now than it was five years ago?
- Who are the target customers and audiences for this market?

If you answer each of these points with about three sentences, then you are already 90% finished with your macro research!

Conducting Macro Industry Research
Step 3: Identify the Most Impactful Industry Drivers
Now you need to identify the biggest drivers and factors that will impact the industry for the next five years. That should include things that will impact the industry positively as well as negatively. For example, do most apparel businesses in the space source materials from China? If so, how might future import and export tax changes impact costs for businesses in this space?

Or for food-service businesses, how might changes in the Food and Drug Administration's policies impact how the industry is able to grow? Or how are food-service businesses affected by culture, and how might health trends impact whether people choose out-of-house dining over cooking at home in the future? There are always potential factors in any industry, and here, your mission is to pick the top three to five factors that would make an impact on your space.

Extra Content Is Appendix Material

Here is the biggest nagging question entrepreneurs have about their research: How much is enough?

From my experience and based on feedback from investors and underwriters, "enough" is 500–1,000 words, or one to three pages.

You should have a ton of extra information from your time digging through your industry. That is a good thing. The more you know about your industry, the more informed you will be to make smart business decisions. However, that does not mean you should dump *everything* you find into your business plan.

The answer to how much you should research is as much as you need to understand what trends happened in your industry five years ago and what experts predict in your industry in three to five years. Then take that information and add it concisely to your macro research section.

If you want to keep additional information or extra details handy, then add them to the Appendix section at the end of your business plan. That section can contain any reports, professional analyses, and other large amounts of data you want to keep attached to your business plan. Keeping these items in the back can help avoid extra length and bloat in your core document but will still keep the additional information handy for you and any other readers.

Don't Get Stuck Over- or "Underresearching"

If you opt for a polished report from a source such as IBISWorld, know that copy and paste is a bad approach. It will be a complete waste of your time because you are skipping the chance to interpret the information critically. This is a surefire way to under-research. Instead, rewrite what you find in shorter, easy-to-understand sentences. And cite your sources in the References section so you can research and reference certain points later if needed.

Things to Avoid

Try to avoid listing any uncited facts or pieces of information. This section of your business plan is not about your gut instinct; it's about facts. I have seen smart, knowledgeable business owners make the mistake of creating a brain dump of everything they think they know about their industry and plopping it into the Research section of their business plan.

This section should be pulled 100 percent from your research, *not* from your knowledge of the industry. Most businesses are a bit detached from or unaware of one or more of their environments (macro, micro, or niche). That is the purpose of this research exercise, to reveal those blind spots.

For inventions, innovations, or disruptor businesses, there may be some triangulation from two or more industries to create a great view of your business potential in a "new" market. Try not to under-research because you feel like nothing out there suits your true industry. Pick a couple of industries that are close or related and trace their trends to see how your business may be affected by those peripheral industries.

You also want to avoid going too far in your research. When I worked my earliest business plans, I accumulated a ton of information. I felt like it made my plan more impressive, made it a greater accomplishment. I wanted people to pick it up and say, "Wow, I bet there's great information in here!" Then I started interviewing bankers and investors. They were honest about how they read business plans or, rather, how they skim business plans.

Then it was obvious: No one wants to read that much information, so why write that much?

As you approach this section, consider stating "this matters because" after every fact or piece of information you include. That can help you stay focused on only the data that is most important. If you can't find a reason that something matters, then it is likely safe to leave it out.

Technical Layout

The Research section can be one of the most boring parts of your entire business plan. The monotony creeps in pretty fast if you aren't careful. To avoid this, try the following tips:

- Make every sentence as short as possible. Aim for impact, not volume.
- Consider adding text boxes that hold important but peripheral stats that you think are important. If you have a list of statistics, consider a bulleted format to make them easier to read.

Macro Analysis

Pajama Business LLC

Sleepwear is classified into the following three market industries:

> Lingerie
> Infants' and Children's Clothing
> Women's Wear

Below is an overview of sleepwear trends in the lingerie store space.

Sleepwear in Lingerie Stores

There are two key drivers for the lingerie store industry: disposable income and the number of adults aged 20 to 64.

Revenue for the lingerie store industry is expected to grow 1 percent over five years to $9.5 billion, according to IBISWorld. In lingerie stores, sleepwear accounts for more than 50 percent of the industry's revenue (O'Connor, 2018). The industry is in a growth cycle, and new stores are expected to launch in the next five years to meet the forecast demand.

Larger department stores are becoming less of a threat to boutique owners who carry limited inventory and often have higher retail prices. Smaller stores are able to cater to a specific niche of highly unique and specialized lingerie and sleepwear solutions, which creates a loyal customer base. In order for lingerie stores to compete with larger department store offerings, many small business owners are turning to local sources from clothes makers who offer direct delivery.

Lingerie Store Industry Revenues
(Source: IBISWorld Report OD4221)

Year	Revenue $ million	Growth %
2003	5,735.7	0.0
2004	5,884.6	2.6
2005	5,772.9	-1.9
2006	5,879.7	1.9
2007	6,026.1	2.5
2008	5,851.0	-2.9
2009	5,667.9	-3.1
2010	5,942.2	4.8
2011	6,432.0	8.2
2012	7,028.6	9.3
2013	7,312.2	4.0
2014	7,752.2	6.0
2015	8,375.3	8.0
2016	8,819.3	5.3
2017	8,909.6	1.0
2018	9,014.3	1.2
2019	9,091.5	0.9
2020	9,168.1	0.8
2021	9,247.7	0.9
2022	9,340.0	1.0
2023	9,477.1	1.5
2024	9,608.8	1.4

Lingerie Stores
Product Segmentation
(Source: IBISWorld Report OD4221)

41%
50%
39%

- Sleepwear Lingerie
- Bras, Girdles, Corsets
- Hosiery, Socks, Tights

You may also consider turning every statistic you can into a chart, table, or graph. That creates a huge benefit, helps you internalize the data, and improves readability for your business plan. If you simply dump tons of information in word form onto a page, it will be difficult to read. It will be skimmed by your audience, or it will be meaningless information for you later.

You should also be careful when it comes to vague or opinion-based language. Avoid the narrative of how "great" or "big" or "strong" your market is. Instead, speak in the third person about the trends and tendencies and how businesses in general can succeed in this space. You'll get more specific about your business and how it will play within the industry in the next sections, but this section should be as unbiased as possible, exclusively a birds-eye view of what is happening.

This way, you can see more organically how you can best fit into the space and meet an existing need. You will also build upon this foundational information in the next two sections. It forces you to see how you are allowing the demand to drive supply. That helps you avoid creating a business that is not meeting clear demand, a problem that is usually amplified by a business owner's blind passion.

Finishing the Traffic SAMS™ Business Plan

Working with Milo and Omar on the Traffic SAMS™ business plan, I clearly realized that they knew their industry inside and out. They had a strong awareness of what their competition was doing, where the macro market was heading, and how to approach it strategically. Their need, like

Market Research – Macro Analysis

Message Board Sign Market

While the largest market share for the message board industry is held by Daktronics, less than 10 percent of the company revenues are from variable message boards that would be competitive to TrafficSAMS™. Other providers such as ADDCO and WANCO would be examples of direct competition in the space. This competition entertains customers that TrafficSAMS™ is targeting, such as players in construction, aero (airports), theme parks, and public event hosts.

Variable Message Signage - Industry Snapshot in 2016
- $4.9B Revenue
- $249.2M Profit
- 6.0% Annual Growth (2011–2016)
- Largest Market Share: Daktronics
- Growth: Profit Margins to be 6% of industry revenue by 2021, up from 5.1% in 2016

Stats from McGinley, 2016 (IbisWorld Industry Report)

Three segments of the message board industry are seen as a stable source for market health: federal transportation spending (budget allocation), private sector nonresidential construction, and growth in air travel. Where government spending has decreased slightly by about 1 percent from 2015 to 2016, the trend is reversing in 2017 as growth will be 0.7 percent by 2021 in state and local government sectors for transportation, counterbalanced by more than 3 percent growth in the aero and construction industry forecasts for 2017 thru 2021 (McGinley, 2016).

Equipment Rental Market: Holistic

With such an important portion of TrafficSAMS™ sales being from rental providers, it is important to understand the health of the rental equipment industry. United Rentals has been strategically chosen as a preferred rental company to partner with for initial TrafficSAMS™ distribution. Based on a 2016 market report from Yengst Associates, United Rentals has been named the largest rental company, owning 13 percent of the North American rental market for equipment.

so many other entrepreneurs, was to figure out a way to get that information onto paper in a meaningful way. Their ability to tell me what they knew about the industry was crucial. It helped me see very quickly that they knew more than the average start-up. It also helped reveal that the research reports provided were not going to do justice to the business plan.

When I worked on their business plan, it was really hard for me to decide to start from scratch on the research. At first, almost defiantly, I tried to leverage the research provided. After all, those were valuable reports, and the information was credible; but it simply wasn't a perfect fit for the context of the business plan. I wasted a lot of time trying to make use of those reports before I finally opted to rely more heavily on manual research.

In the end, I'm so glad I finally took the new approach, even though it took a bit longer to gather everything needed. The research was robust and thorough. There was a lot of information to include, but the business plan was condensed and investor-ready in the end.

Don't Get Stuck: How to Get Started

For the first steps, try to focus more on reading than writing. As you begin, try to avoid feeling overwhelmed by aiming to get just a small list of research options jotted down. Start by finding your NAICS code, and then pick three to five sources you might use to start looking for information. Visit them one at a time and see if you can find one piece of useful information in each website or report. As you continue, you will find answers to the core questions your Macro Industry research section needs to include.

When you finish this section, you will be ready to get more granular. You will be in a position to drill down into the micro industry where your business will operate. That will require a bit more research, but it may feel more comfortable to you since you may find that you are dealing with more familiar information.

My Macro Industry Research Section includes:

- ❑ My NAICS code
- ❑ The size and projected growth for my industry
- ❑ The most impactful industry drivers for my business

Chapter 4

Micro Industry

Honestly, market research can either go really good, or really bad. You can either get really excited about everything out there, and how there are gaps with other providers and how you can offer a differentiation.

Or you can get really depressed if you can't see the differentiators between your products or services and others on the market. Either way, it's all about what you decide to do with that information.

—Paul Roberson, founder of FLO

https://www.flodoggie.com/

Paul Roberson contacted me about a proprietary belt invention. His invention is one of those things where you see the product and you just *know* you need it. So once I saw the picture of what he created, I was absolutely itching to support the business plan.

Paul's company is called FLO. Under this brand, he created a belt with a ball bearing system that allows the wearer to have hands-free control of whatever is attached. One core use for the product is to leverage it for dog walking. However, the belt was very versatile and could be used for applications ranging from more practical utility belts for construction workers, more accessible belts for members of law enforcement, and more flexible carrying solutions for photo and filming professionals.

Paul needed a business plan that would attract investors. He started building the plan, pitching deck, and financials on his own. Soon, he ran into issues with time and needed clarity on what investors would look for. Since he was juggling a full-time job while trying to launch the business, he found himself at a common entrepreneurial crossroad: He simply needed help.

I felt elated when we began working together. As a dog owner who has experienced challenges walking my own two dogs in a tangle of leashes, I personally loved the design of his belt and was quick to volunteer to be one of FLO's earliest consumers. One thing became clear, though: This was *not* just a dog belt. This was a cross-industry invention that had huge potential beyond simplifying life for pet owners. However, I wasn't sure whether diving into those other industries in the business plan was the right approach.

Have you ever experienced a time in the middle of a conversation where you knew more information about something but weren't sure whether to share it? Perhaps you didn't know if the people in the group would grasp what you were trying to explain or if they would just see it as too much information. Or maybe you wondered if it was appropriate to go into more detail in case the others saw that as great information to know. That was how I felt about the business plan for FLO. I was treading between need to know, good to know, and too much information.

The challenge with the FLO business plan was its versatility. The exact thing that made it so amazing—its wide application of use—was what made the business plan so hard to finalize. In fact, Paul had been battling this for months. He even landed on developing two separate website concepts: one for dog walking and another for other applications. Now I had to gauge the right option. Should we consolidate these business niches and focus on launching the overarching brand or keep going with a focus on market entry based on the product application for pet owners?

Let Me Be Honest with You

Moving into the Micro Research section of your business plan is like tackling a lawn filled with weed patches. You need to be very careful about how you distribute weed killer. You don't want to cover everything, only the patches of interest. Otherwise, it is literally overkill, and you may cover far more than you actually intended and hurt the quality of your lawn. It is the same situation with your business plan. You may be excited to cover every aspect of your business potential, but you have to be selective about what to focus on in order to create an effective business plan.

In the end, Paul and I agreed on an approach. We targeted the business plan based on entry into the pet space. Our market research—the macro and micro trend information—and competitive landscaping focused solely on the pet industry. However, when we talked about market entry in the business plan, we also made it clear that this was Phase 1 and that future phases would lead down other usage paths for the utility belt. That was a delicate mention that allowed investors to see the growth potential without diving totally into a new business model and launching strategy that would need to accompany those other market entry goals.

It is important to have a clear focus by the time you reach this section in your business plan. The Micro Research section is where you will need to dig more deeply into the business space, so you want to make sure you are focusing on the right business sector. As you research, you may have to consider some hard truths that may be uncomfortable. You will need to venture beyond what you think you know about your business space and actively seek out the things that could cause business failure. You are looking for problems with your business plan. Your mind may fight you and tell you there's nothing that would negatively impact your business. However, if you want to succeed, you need to face reality. You need to broaden your awareness and find problems now so you can prepare a game plan to address them proactively.

The Goal of Your Micro Industry Research

This chapter will guide you through conducting a thorough analysis to help you focus on the right topics in your Micro Industry research. This section of your business plan is all about uncovering market factors that may affect you. The Macro Research you conducted in the last chapter showed the broader industry trends, but now you need to focus on what micro conditions may impact your business directly. The Micro Research section is something that demands you to be honest and ask some of the following questions:

> What don't I know?
> What could put me out of business?
> What are the most powerful elements that could make or break my success?

While these questions are running through your mind, you should remain externally focused. Step away from your role as creator of the business so you can see things as unbiased as humanly possible. It can feel counterintuitive, but a huge portion of a business plan is not even about the actual business; it's about external factors that will eventually impact the business. Keep that in mind in this section in particular.

Impact of This Section for Investors

Investors will review this section for an understanding of your thought process. They will not only consider the information but also how the information was interpreted. They will consider how you analyze trends. They will watch for signs that you take a proactive approach to addressing potential risks. That will influence their ability to trust you to be independent with management and strategy decisions as the business moves forward.

With Paul's business plan, I was looking to show investors that the approach to start with the dog leash market made sense based on market opportunity and lower barrier to entry. Paul and I talked at length about the other options for FLO, and it wasn't until I finished the research portions of the business plan that I was completely in agreement that branding specifically for the dog leash market would be highly feasible to start with. Since the research supported that conclusion, investors would be able to reach the same interpretation as they reviewed the research in the business plan.

Impact of This Section for Bankers

This section will be used to understand additional risk factors that exist for your business. It will show investors how great your external threats are and whether you are positioning your business to survive those threats. It will also be a way for underwriters to have a more in-depth understanding of your industry, which will have an impact on banks' appetite for your business in their portfolios.

Impact of This Section for Strategy

This section will serve as a way to gain clarity of your business strategy. When you uncover factors that will have possible impacts for your business, you create solutions before the problems occur. Often, this turns into an exercise that changes core elements of your business. The reason this is important is because of timing. Handling your external factors now is easier to do at a foundational level before you build your business. Finding highly impactful external factors in years two or five could mean that you need to restructure huge strategy pillars in your business, which could be difficult when your business is already fully operational.

Creating Your Micro Industry Analysis

This is a progressive point in your business plan. You know your general industry, and now you can research the more immediate arena. This is when you examine the space where you and your competitors will operate, but avoid mentioning competitors for now.

One of the simplest ways to complete a Micro Analysis is to perform a STEEPLE[3] Analysis. That will guide you to work through social, technological, economic, environmental, political, legal, and ethical factors that may influence your business. The following sections will show you how to think about each factor and the ways you can consider applying them to your business situation.

STEEPLE Factor 1: Social Considerations

The social factors that impact your business are related to cultural trends. For example, let's consider the social factors that impact food and beverage businesses. These providers have to pay attention to how people *feel* about food. Since the colonies were established in America, there have been clear waves of social influence over food and dietary trends. When the population changes with each new generation, when there are new trends in immigrant populaces, and even when new fad diets and scientific declarations about nutrition appear, there are shifts in what is considered good or bad to eat.[4] Being aware of what is shifting is important so you can plan to adjust your business offerings accordingly.

Social factors also influence other industries. Think of the terms *made in America, a portion of the proceeds go to charitable causes, environmentally green*, and other slogans that are meant to tell you about the cultural principles of a company. When businesses display these declarations, they are tapping into a specific social factor to reach aligned buyers.

As a consumer, you may have experienced positive social factors in a company that influenced your buying decisions. Have you ever

---

3. "Differences between STEEP and STEEPLE Analysis," *Pestle Analysis*, (February 13, 2015), http://pestleanalysis.com/steep-and-steeple-analysis/.
4. R. Pillsbury, *No Foreign Food* (New York: Routledge, 1998).

decided to become a customer of a brand partly because you liked the company's cause or mission? Was there ever a time when you felt like a business really had clear values and you personally felt aligned with its purpose? Perhaps you gravitated to a company that donates a portion of its proceeds to a charity or closes and gives employees paid holidays off despite those days being their most profitable business days. That is an example of how a company works with social factors in its business.

See where social culture may touch your business and look into where those cultural trends may be going in the future. Some trends are worth addressing and catering to as a competitive edge, and some trends simply are not aligned with your business, and that is fine. You want to focus on the trends that align with your core audience and consider how you can communicate to them that you are socially aligned with their interests.

STEEPLE Factor 2: Technological Considerations

Technology trends are ever-changing and directly impact most, if not every, business. Technology considerations go beyond physical devices and Internet usage. In an online world, technological factors include how we operate daily. For brick-and-mortar stores, that includes changes in how we process payments, how we follow up with customers, and how we attract new customers.

Upcoming changes are not limited to digital businesses. It's no surprise that physical stores are using technology more than ever, especially for marketing. Many physical establishments are using "beacon marketing."[5] In its simplest form, beacon marketing is tracking who is near your business and sending them instant promotions, coupons, or other alerts on their mobile devices, encouraging them to stop in and visit your business storefront. It is changing the landscape of how many businesses compete in their marketing.

---

5. "Systems and Methods for Delivering Proximity-Based Marketing Content to Mobile Devices," *Google Patents*, https://patents.google.com/patent/US20120047011A1/en.

What does that mean for you? It means you need to create awareness for yourself on how to use technology to your benefit. Maybe beacon marketing is an awesome tool to research and consider. Maybe you will do some research and see that there is a gap in mobile apps in your industry, and you are considering using a mobile app to help your business stand out in the market. Maybe your research reveals a rising social media platform that isn't widely popular yet but has users who are in your target audience.

It's important to discover and find these possible options now during your business plan effort so you can consider how they fit into your business strategy. It also means you need to know how technology changes in the near future may require you to pivot.

STEEPLE Factor 3: Economic Considerations

Depending on where you search online, you may see in the STEEPLE Analysis a bit of mixing in the concepts for political and economic factors. For instance, some sources consistently list taxes, trade, and legal policy under political or economic factors. However, for your business plan, use the economic section of your Micro Analysis to evaluate the *buyer* market.

Typically, the range of influence for economic factors happens on a global or national level. Large-scale factors such as an impending recession, an increase in unemployment, or an increase in foreclosure rates can impact your customers and change their spending habits. Focus on the factors that directly affect your ideal customers and their ability to buy from you during the next one to three years.

STEEPLE Factor 4: Environmental Considerations

The environmental factors in a business can be slightly abstract, depending on the industry. For businesses in agriculture, obvious environmental factors include predictions in weather patterns, including impending droughts and volatile seasons. For businesses supplying products related to environmental conditions such as household air filters and water purification systems, the environmental factors include air and water quality in the regions where target customers are located.

However, for other businesses, environmental factors can be less clear. Try to envision your day-to-day operations one year from now. What components are in place? How can aspects of environmental factors impact you in this future vision?

STEEPLE Factor 5: Political Considerations

For some industries, political considerations will be obvious. Operations for businesses in agriculture, defense, and any industry can be directly impacted by government policy or spending. But the not-so-obvious impacts are usually the ones that cause the most damage.

Changes in taxes on imported steel can mean the metal hardware in your new invention may be more expensive than you thought, destroying your profit margins. For Paul's business strategy, he planned to manufacture in the United States. He's learned about upcoming trade tariff changes domestically and internationally. He recognized that some trade implications would impact the steel and nylon materials in his product. Even though the tariff increases weren't an issue yet, he was aware that the impacts of those political moves could increase the costs of his products. These were important elements to be mindful of early in the business planning phase.

Try to think critically about what could touch your business. Find at least two factors at the federal level and two at the state level that could impact your business. Discuss how changes in those factors could impact your business positively or negatively.

STEEPLE Factor 6: Legal Considerations

Legal implications for your business will exist no matter your business type. Common internal things to consider revolve around how you will handle returns, disputes, or customer issues. Considering external issues—your core focus in this section—can be a broad task. Local requirements and possible changes in city or county permit requirements may mean that the huge, bright new sign you wanted to order for your storefront will no longer be in compliance with local ordinances if a new proposition is approved. Legal requirements that govern antidiscrimination, hiring practices, collection of unemployment taxes, and so on will all impact your business if they shift. Visit your local Chamber of Commerce for the latest and greatest, even if you have an online business.

Another legal consideration most new businesses overlook relates to customer information. For any business that wants to connect with customers, it is likely that there will be a collection of customer data at some level. That may include collecting and storing e-mail addresses, physical mailing addresses, payment preferences, and site pixels so you can market to people who have visited your website. Collection of any kind of data means you must understand how you are legally responsible to protect that information. That includes data privacy laws in the United States and abroad. As a starting point, consider getting familiar with policies such as the General Data Protection Regulation (GDPR).

Beyond digital legalities, you have plenty of other legal issues that will impact your business. Identify at least five external legal factors that could impact your business and research them to discover any proposed changes to those policies. Impending changes can damage your business if you aren't aware of them. By broadening your awareness now, you will be ahead of the game and able to watch for the changes and be prepared for them if they ever occur.

STEEPLE Factor 7: Ethical Considerations

The ethical factors in business touch your internal operation and how your business operates within the context of society. This idea can scare a lot of first-time business owners, but applying critical thinking can help simplify it a bit. Think critically about the effects of ethical behaviors your business will have, such as the following:

- How your managers interact with your employees.
  Example: Do employees get adequate overtime pay, days off, and shift durations?
- How your employees interact with your customers.
  Example: Do employees treat all customers fairly, equally, and respectfully?

- How your customers interact with your products and services.
  Example: Do your customers face any risk, harm, or danger when using or consuming your product or service?
- How your business interacts with suppliers, providers, and creators of your products and services.
  Example: Does your business work with suppliers who offer a quality guarantee on their products or services?
- How your suppliers, providers, and creators interact with the products and services you sell.
  Example: Does your business work with suppliers who follow fair labor laws to produce your products?

Many of the aspects of acting ethically are in parallel with the concepts of corporate social responsibility. Simply put, this means you are looking at all angles of your business to try to create as much ethical awareness as possible so you can be a positive factor on society as a whole. You want to answer this question: If someone wanted to find something wrong with our integrity in the way we run our business, could they find something?

There's always something that can be considered when it comes to ethics. That doesn't mean you have to donate all profits to charity or pay all your employees higher-than-average wages. It simply means you need to be aware of possible areas of exposure and ask yourself if addressing these issues proactively would align with your business's level of commitment to ethical standards.

Things to Avoid

Try to avoid making this section long-winded. You do not need seven pages to represent each STEEPLE component. You may jot down plenty of notes and create lots of great insights, but you don't necessarily want to cram them all into your main business plan. Instead, consider including only one to three sentences that address each STEEPLE component, and put those points in paragraph form. Any additional analysis, facts, or explanation should be added as an Appendix to your business plan.

Technical Layout

As you develop the key takeaways of your STEEPLE Analysis, you will want to end with a clear purpose. You should make sure all insights from your STEEPLE Analysis are useful and actionable. To accomplish this, take a minimum of three of the biggest factors and create a SMART goal for each. The SMART goal you create should address or shield your business from the negative effects of those factors. SMART goals are goals that are specific, measurable, achievable, results-focused, and time-bound.[6]

Micro Analysis

Pajama Business LLC

The operating space has several external factors to consider. These factors are considered within the direct industry in which the business operates. These may influence the business, and are analyzed below via a STEEPLE analysis.

Social Factors

The social factors affecting Pajama Business LLC include the movement for work at home professionals. These employees may need to attend video conference calls from time to time, where their torso is required to show work-appropriate attire, even though they are out of the office. For this reason, we have included the following SMART goal for our first year of production:

Goal: By month 12, add a loungewear "Professional" pajama line where tops meet most business-casual dress code requirements.

Technological Factors

Many loungewear customers in a recent survey note that phone-holding pockets in their pajamas is a strong desire. Between pockets being too small, or pajama components being too loose to store a phone comfortably without risk of falling out or dropping, many pajama wearers opt to hold the phone in hand. 60% of survey respondents cite this as an inconvenience or a nuisance. As phone technology trends are showing mobile devices growing in dimension, and some even growing in weight, we recognize that our products should be capable of adapting to those size differences. We also want to be mindful not to create bulky pockets with excessive fabric, and would like to include tech-ready features like headphone or charger cut-outs in phone pockets for wearers.

Goal: Within the main product line, before the 6th round of production, create prototype for new mobile-ready pockets and explore patent potential.

The New York Times published survey results last year showing that 43% of employed Americans worked remotely at least on occasion (New York Times, 2017).

---

6. A. Shahin and M.A. Mahbod, "Prioritization of Key Performance Indicators: An Integration of Analytical Hierarchy Process and Goal Setting," *International Journal of Productivity and Performance Management* 56:3, 226–240.

For instance, you may recognize a possible problem with ethical factors when you envision employee interactions with customers. Perhaps having above-average customer service is a way you hope to differentiate your business, and therefore, fostering a high ethical standard for how your employees treat customers is your highest priority. You can turn this into a SMART goal as follows:

> Goal: Each employee is required to successfully pass (above 70 percent) a two-week awareness training program before working one-on-one with customers.

Is this goal specific? Yes. Employees are required to take a specific training to increase awareness and establish interaction expectations with customers.

Is this goal measurable? Yes. Employees have to pass an awareness training program (70 percent or higher) in order to proceed.

Is this goal attainable? Yes. Local training programs are affordable and accessible for off-site training of each employee.

Is this goal results-focused? Yes. This goal will lead to the ultimate result of well-trained employees who understand the integrity expectations of their roles with customers.

Is this goal time-bound? Yes. Employees have two weeks to complete the training in order to be able to proceed in the role.

By incorporating SMART goals into your Micro Industry section, you are proactively analyzing and mitigating risk for your business. You are also creating an easy way to focus your own research efforts. Once you have a clear SMART goal to apply to a factor, you can consider that a good transition point for moving on to the next factor.

Finishing the FLO Business Plan

An area where Paul stood out from any other client was his understanding of external factors. He knew clearly that he was entering a space where other influences were in play, some of which he couldn't even see. Instead of ignoring those influences, he worked to understand them the

The pet industry will continue to prosper as more businesses begin to offer services to customers who are accompanied by their furry companions. Pets are becoming more widely accepted by the public as household family members. Based on that notion, restaurants, airports, and hospitals are accepting pets more, regardless of whether they are service animals.

Social

The increasing humanization of pets, health-conscious owners, and owners' attraction to new innovative products have changed market trends contributing to the driving demand for pet supplies. In fact, market data has shown that pet owners are treating their pets much like their own children by buying them luxury gifts, celebrating their birthdays, or buying them seasonal outfits. This sense of loyalty and commitment is particularly strong among dog owners.

Ethical

Noted by the *Animal Wellness Magazine*, the APPA 2015–2016 report shows that more places of business are catering to pets, with 8 percent of pet owners reporting that their workplace allows pets, 28 percent of dog owners have been to a pet-friendly hotel, and 9 percent have dined at a pet-friendly restaurant. These high traffic areas present challenges to traditional leashes as pet owners will prefer products that afford them more control and stability without sacrificing flexibility.

Technological

Pet owners are also becoming more interested in pet technologies, and products such as wearable technology and luxury pet items are both seeing surges in demand. FLO capitalizes on both trends with a novel and attractive form factor while also solving the issues posed by traditional leashes.

Consumer Segmentation by Age

- Consumers 25–34
- Consumers 35–44
- Consumers 45–54
- Consumers 55–64
- Consumers 65–74

Although consumers of all ages are prone to spend on pets, those 45 and older (including Baby Boomers) are expected to designate more disposable income to pets instead of dependent children as they become focused on health, wellness, and emotional comfort of themselves and their pets (Oliver, 2017).

Reported by petfoodindustry.com, findings from the 2015–2016 National Pet Owners Survey include an increase in the number of new and younger pet owners. The study found that more than 10 percent of pet owners are new pet owners which equates to almost 8 million new pet owners within the past year.

best he could. He focused on protecting himself, patenting his product, and taking time to clarify risks that might affect his business.

When finalizing his business plan, the focus in the research was 100 percent on the target micro market: all things "dog leash." It was hard for me to finish this section because we were still actively talking about the other applications for his invention. So, factors that would affect the FLO product in law enforcement application or construction use were not included in the business plan. To keep it singularly focused was a real challenge because of the wide potential for the FLO belt.

At times, it seemed impossible to answer certain parts of the STEEPLE Analysis for FLO. My mind would glaze, and I would draw a blank on how to research and analyze for one factor or another. But this was usually just a sign that my brain needed a break, and sure enough, I could finish the next day after a good night of sleep and a quick mental reset.

For the Micro Industry section, you may be inclined to brush over this part. To be honest, this is one of the most intense sections for me to finish in each of my business plans. It isn't that it is hard, per se; it's just that it requires a lot of mental energy to do it correctly. It can be really easy to gloss over each section, write vague thoughts, or make connections that are a bit far-fetched. That is why pacing yourself is key.

Don't Get Stuck: How to Get Started

I recommend that you tackle this section in pieces with structured time breaks between each factor you work through. The reason for this is that it can be hard to pivot from thinking about environmental factors for an hour and then working on legal factors for the next hour. Instead of making that hard pivot, your brain may find it easier to stay on its original focus.

I often find I can breeze through, say, the ethical section, and then I get stuck on the social factors. I often draw a complete blank with that kind of pivot because my brain hasn't had time to switch gears from ethical to social. It's a whole new perspective to consider, and giving your brain time—a few hours or a few days—to shift into the new focus can be helpful.

As you move past the Micro Industry research, you are ready to dive into a critique of your competitors. The next chapter will guide you through developing your Competitive Analysis. This portion of your business plan will focus on what other operators are doing in your space.

My Micro Industry Analysis includes:

- ❏ STEEPLE Factor(s) 1: Social considerations & one related SMART goal

- ❏ STEEPLE Factor(s) 2: Technological considerations & one related SMART goal

- ❏ STEEPLE Factor(s) 3: Economic considerations & one related SMART goal

- ❏ STEEPLE Factor(s) 4: Environmental considerations & one related SMART goal

- ❏ STEEPLE Factor(s) 5: Political considerations & one related SMART goal

- ❏ STEEPLE Factor(s) 6: Legal considerations & one related SMART goal

- ❏ STEEPLE Factor(s) 7: Ethical considerations & one related SMART goal

Chapter 5

Competitive Analysis

It's such a critical piece of the puzzle to honestly look at who competitors are. Really getting in there. That's part of the process of understanding the market and how we would really fit. And we looked critically at, A), what don't we want to be, and B), what do we want to be.

—Mark Lewis, co-founder of HelloCecil

https://hellocecil.com/

▶ hellocecil

M ark Lewis, co-founder of HelloCecil, first reached out just before the holiday season. I am always a bit careful to avoid booking too many business plans during the holidays since my bandwidth is a bit thin that time of year. But with Mark, it was a no-brainer. His business plan was definitely going to be one of the projects I would work to finish before Thanksgiving. Once I understood his vision, I couldn't help but get excited to support him.

Mark and his co-founder are the brains behind a new business called HelloCecil. The company offers software as a service (SaaS). Its core product is an automated video interviewing software designed for small and medium-sized businesses. It was created to help smaller business teams execute talent selection and hiring without a robust human resources department. I recognized right away that HelloCecil was different from other options on the market in both its simplicity and accessibility. Thanks to its friendly and intuitive interface, it had the potential for broader future applications in the likes of education and talent casting.

The business plan for HelloCecil would be used for strategy purposes at first. Later, it would be leveraged for fund-raising in future phases of the business launch. Mark and his co-founder were involved in self-funding activities initially. They collaborated and managed things from afar, with Mark in Los Angeles and his co-founder in Rhode Island. Despite their distance, these co-founders clearly synced well and were following the right steps to launch this new SaaS business.

Since I support small business owners as a large portion of my client base, not to mention firsthand experiences with hiring struggles at my husband's car wash business, I saw the value in HelloCecil. The market opportunity for this one-way video solution was definitely present. Mark and his co-founder had done a fantastic job with their research and had already mapped their competitive landscape. In fact, when I reviewed the work they had done on their competitors, I was faced with a rare question: Do I really need to touch this, or is it perfect as is?

Have you ever been faced with a situation where you weren't sure something was really a problem? Perhaps you stared at an e-mail you were drafting, wondering if you should add more or just leave it alone. Maybe you even saw an optional software update on your phone, but you questioned whether you really wanted to upgrade for fear that you would regret the new features. I felt this way with Mark's competitive section of his business plan. It was already very well drafted, and I wasn't sure any changes were really necessary.

The hardest part about the HelloCecil business plan was making sure I left the integrity of the great work already completed. Yet I also needed to round out and fill in gaps where they existed. Sometimes, though, it's hard to see where gaps exist when you didn't build the research yourself to begin with. This meant I would need to retrace some of their research steps to be able to finish the plan fully.

Let Me Be Honest with You

The Competitive Analysis section of your business plan can be downright fun to put together. It is where you can uncover competitor weaknesses and feel empowered about your own business venture. However, it also needs to be a place where you find balanced insights about your competition. You need to be able to be honest about their best and worst qualities. Sometimes, this can be harder to do than you might imagine. Your natural bias can kick in and want to focus on your competitors' bad qualities, but you have to try to stay as objective as possible.

In the end, I did leave HelloCecil's core competitor analysis intact. The reason Mark's analysis was so impressive was because he went the extra mile to get deep and direct impressions of how his competitors were performing. He came away with some negatives on where the competition could improve, but more impressively, he found a ton of great things his competitors were doing in the space.

He didn't obsess over another company's bad practices and neither did he focus on beating them at their own game. Instead, he focused on filling specific gaps that existed in the market. He made it less about being better than the competition and more about stepping into a new niche altogether since other providers already serviced their niches well enough.

The Goal of Your Competitive Analysis

Your Competitive Analysis is meant to outline the current players and the state of your niche market. It will create a scenario where you can clearly see a gap or need that your business will be able to fill. It is also a place where you can explain where your competitors are doing great things—things you may want to adopt in your own business.

My challenge in this section of the HelloCecil business plan was simply to make sure they were viewing the competitive landscape fairly.

After all, a skewed competitor review can shift the success potential of a business strategy. It has to be done from an honest and neutral perspective.

When you develop the Niche Industry and Competitive Analysis section of your business plan, you will want to look for those providers who make you uncomfortable. Try not to seek the reasons you are *better* than your competition. That will lead to a really slanted view of reality. When you focus on the providers in your space, analyze their best *and* worst traits. You can then create a game plan. You can be the right combination of their best features, without their worst issues, and still bring a unique spin to your product or service. That is what will make you a dominant player in the space.

Impact of This Section for Investors

Investors will see this section as an indicator of true market demand. They will also look for clear indicators that show this market has room for a new entrant. Some kind of simple table or visual to help show where there are gaps in existing providers will be greatly appreciated by investors so they can understand where there is a hole that your business can fill in the market.

Impact of This Section for Bankers

Bankers will watch this section to gauge proximity of threat. They want to see that there are other providers in the industry doing something very similar to your business. But they also want to see that those providers are somehow not already servicing your target audience. Sometimes, this is a location-specific analysis. Is there another restaurant, laundromat, or convenience store near where you plan to put your restaurant, laundromat, or convenience store? What niche angle are those providers missing that you could capitalize on?

Sometimes, this is an analysis on offering. Are other providers all servicing a market with the exception of one thing? If they decide to start providing that one thing in the future, is it possible for your business to provide a better version of it?

Impact of this Section for Strategy

Your strategy will be relatively clear after completing this section. You will know what the broader market trends look like, what micro market patterns and threats exist, and what other current businesses are providing in the space. With clarity on how other businesses are doing and where they are excelling or failing, you can think critically about your own entry strategy and thus find success.

With HelloCecil, Mark was looking for strategy validation. He wanted to make sure he was being neutral in his research and business plan approach. He recognized the value of having a strategy review from an outside perspective. So for that reason, I was very diligent as I looked for indicators that he was wrong or missing something in his business vision. Fortunately, Mark had researched, analyzed, and critiqued his own business model so well and so thoroughly that there were no big surprises to present with the final business plan, especially when it came to the Competitive Analysis section.

The following will walk you through how to complete this section with research and a simple comparison table. When you work through this section, try to avoid mental barriers. Your mind may try to overlook the real threats that make you uncomfortable. It may try to keep you out of the weeds and away from the details of what the competition is doing. Try to view this as if you were a reporter or an investigator looking to uncover the real story of how each of your competitors is doing—the good and the bad.

This is not a time to think about solutions. Try not to let your own business be your focus. Right now, it's about understanding your niche industry and the players who will serve as your greatest competition.

Creating Your Competitive Analysis

To create your Competitive Analysis, you will research what others are doing, how they are doing it, and what is and isn't working for them. This exercise typically leads to several aha moments about the competition. This level of clarity will directly impact your business.

Looking at your competitors objectively can be one of the hardest parts of a business plan. Most people botch this by simply writing what they think they know instead of doing fresh digging into what the competition is up to. Or sometimes, they never realize who they truly have as their competition.

This very thing is what contributes to many business failures. Approaching your business with blinders or a purely negative view of the competition can be fatal. You cannot plan for what you cannot see.

Step 1 in Creating a Competitive Analysis: List the Knowns

To start your Competitive Analysis, you need to jot down who your competitors are and what you know about them. You will use this as a starting point. As you look at the list of what you think you know about your competitors, also note whether there is anything specific you don't know. When you research, your goal will be to validate the things you know and try to find answers to additional questions.

If you already know your competition on some level, that is likely where you will feel most comfortable—staying where you are already familiar and knowledgeable. Many business owners are well aware of their immediate competition. In order to dive a bit deeper and make sure you know what matters most, this section guides you to create a table with specific details on your closest competitors. You will also remain hyper-focused on your most direct and immediate competitors in this section. That way, your analysis won't become overwhelming or unfocused.

When you move on to Step 2, you will look for other competitors in the space who were not originally on your radar as direct competition but who may technically be part of your competitor landscape. You may come across them now, and it's a good idea to add them to your list for further research in the next step.

Note for Innovative Businesses

If you have ever said, "There is no one else doing this" or "There is no competition for my business," you may be classified as an innovative business. Lots of inventions and disruptor businesses are in this category, and sometimes traditional businesses doing things very differently are considered innovators as well. However, you need to watch your competition in a slightly more strategic way.

Innovative businesses need to triangulate various parts of their business concept that are similar to existing businesses. No investor or lender will like to hear you say, "My business is 100 percent unlike any other business." They want to see that you are being honest and realistic. They want to see that you are actually putting in the work to understand your market and learn lessons based on successes and failures from related businesses, even if those businesses aren't exactly the same as yours. The process of running your business is going to be similar to *something* that has already been done before. Try to draw parallels, even if another business or product is different from what you are doing.

Step 2 in Creating a Competitive Analysis: Organize the Data

Now that you have an initial list of your familiar competitors, go ahead and organize what you know. You will create a simple visual to help you see gaps in what other providers are doing. To start your comparison, list your competitors in a table format. Each competitor gets a row. If you have more than 10 competitors, only include the details of your 10 closest competitors in your main business plan. List the rest of them in an appendix. That will make your business plan easier to read.

You will start with five columns, although you may need to add more, depending on how many factors you want to analyze. These columns are where you will list the factors that matter, including customer review ratings, things they offer, and things they currently don't offer. Include their prices, their methods of handing returns or refunds, and other components that would make a difference to the customer experience.

If it is feasible, go through the motions of their customer experience by actually inquiring or purchasing from your competition for a true insider's perspective. You may be surprised with what you learn, and you can add even more valuable data to your competitive comparison table.

What you need to add to each column will be determined by your business type. For instance, let's imagine that you want to open a car wash. However, you know a new franchise car wash is already operating down the street. You assume they are too competitive for you to be near. You decide to visit as a customer, and you come away feeling the employees are unfriendly. Once you dig in and see they have terrible reviews online, you add that two-star data point to your competitor table. You also add the top issues shown in negative reviews, such as customer service, prices, or quality.

While doing this, you take note of the most important complaints that the business cannot easily change. For example, customer service can be fluid, so they can change that rather easily with new personnel or training. However, since it is a franchise, quality is hard to change due to existing supplier agreements with soap companies and hardware providers that are negotiated at a franchise level. These quality things are not easily changed by the franchise owner. So that can be a competitive point that benefits your business if you opt to focus on quality.

Do the same with positives. Look for what the customers love about your competitors. See if you can duplicate those in your business. Do this as unbiased as possible and try not to rationalize anything off the table. Just list each item as a positive and note that you may need to consider it later for your own business.

Step 3 in Creating a Competitive Analysis: Expand the View

Now that you have clarity on familiar competitors, challenge yourself to identify a few new competitors. This section is where most people find competitors they had no idea even existed, or they find others who are doing things a little differently, which can serve as inspiration for their own business. Aim to list about three new competitors in your comparison table.

With these new competitors, also think about your first impression when you see their logos, brand colors, price structures, and other elements of their businesses. This fresh view of them can help with your perspective on how you can create the right first impression with the elements in your own business. It's easier to recognize what works and what doesn't when you consider things from a truly unfamiliar vantage point, so your first impression of these additional competitors can be invaluable.

Once you have a full list of competitors—again, no more than 10—offer a brief few sentences about each one in your business plan. In paragraph form, break down the key takeaways about their competitive status in the market. Is one competitor great at customer service but too overpriced to gain real market share? Is another competitor offering an expanded product line that seems to resonate well with buyers? Make these takeaways clear in your writing.

When you create your competitor table, open yourself up to feedback from either someone you trust or a professional who can support you. Consider having a friend, trusted employee, or even a customer help you identify your real competitors. Review your table assumptions aloud with that person and encourage feedback about whether you missed any obvious factors or elements about those competitors. This outside perspective will help you see things more clearly and avoid any overlooked areas you need to include.

Avoid the idea that this is an exercise you only complete once. You should do a quick check every month or every quarter to make sure you understand what your competitors are changing or adjusting. Just as you are continuously trying new things and working to be the best business you can be, so are your competitors. They will be working through trial and error in many ways, just like you. Competition will always be iterating, and you need to watch for the newest shifts so you are prepared.

Here is one note of caution about the language you use. Avoid stating that your product or service does not exist in your competitive space. Whether or not it is true, it is usually very unlikely that something is 100 percent unique in the market. A safer phrase is this: "So far, our closest competitors are…" and then list those. You can talk about why they don't match your offer, but avoid the "does not exist" phrase when you think and write about your competitive landscape.

Technical Layout

Addressing your competitive landscape section should consist of a competitor table and a quick narrative of key takeaways. The table will likely be one-half to a single page in length, and the narrative should take about 400–500 words. The narrative should summarize your findings and outline what you have discovered.

Competitive Analysis   Pajama Business LLC

The following will review the top five competitors for Pajama Business LLC. The key information includes their star ratings, average price point, return period, and core offerings.

	Stars	Average $$	Sizes	Return Period	Core Offerings
Pajama Business	TBD	$15	XS-2X	30 days	Versatile loungewear
Competitor 1	5	$13	S-XL	7 days	Sleep wear & lingerie
Competitor 2	3.5	$22	S-2X	15 days	Loungewear & sweaters
Competitor 3	4.5	$17	XS-XL	15 days	Loungewear & footwear
Competitor 4	3	$15	XS-3X	15 days	Loungewear
Competitor 5	3	$15	XS-2X	30 days	Loungewear & accessories
Competitor 6	2.4	$14	S-XL	15 days	Loungewear & bath items

Competitor 1 Analysis

Competitor 1 is a well established brand with a strong social media following. It has a lot of customer complaints and seems to get a lot of returns. It does well with marketing, but the quality of the product seems to be subpar from customers' perspectives. Worse, it has a shorter return policy than most other providers, so there seems to be dissatisfaction by customers regarding this point as well.

Based on what Competitor 1 is experiencing, we will ensure the right supplier is onboard for good material quality. Will also make sure our return policy is longer than 7 days for customer convenience.

Competitor 2 Analysis

Competitor 2 has been on the scene for about three years and has already undergone a major brand overhaul since launch. It has good star ratings, and the business seems to do well despite having a higher price point. It has an expanded offering of sweaters, and this line seems to be a significant portion of its consumer traffic. It has an active presence on Instagram, which seems to be its favored social channel.

Here are some questions to use as prompts to guide your narrative:

- What are my competitors doing right?
- Can I identify any gaps where they can further improve?
- What are they doing marketing-wise that is unique from others?

- What makes customers buy from them?
- What are the top customer complaints they are receiving?
- What are their price points compared to other competitors?
- How easily could they improve their problem areas?

Along the way, you can opt to add customer logos. That can be a great way to help visualize the landscape. It can also offer perspective in understanding how your business can stand out with branding and design.

Finishing the HelloCecil Business Plan

My goal with supporting Mark in his business plan for HelloCecil was to avoid fixing what wasn't broken. I validated what information I could and looked for other pieces of insights I could add to his analysis. But overall, the goal was to preserve the integrity of the great work Mark and his co-founder had already completed.

▶ hello cecil

Competitor Analysis

The following outlines the immediate competition to HelloCecil.

Company	Feature focus	Unique selling points	Market position	Pricing
HelloCecil	One-way video interviewing only	Platform simplicity; no sales reps or huge support team required; low/simple pricing	Startups/small businesses (less than 250 employees)	Where competitors offer three-tiered pricing, we will be one price, i.e. $149
Competitor	One way and live video interviewing, Scheduling program	Enterprise strength	Focuses on large organization hiring hundreds of people each year	Custom pricing
Competitor	One way and live video interviewing	Enterprise strength; video interviews/assessments/coaching	Large organizations	Programs start at $150k/month
Competitor	Audio/Video interviewing, live interviewing, applicant tracking, video onboarding, scheduling	Offer both options: Candidates can erase/re-record, or be limited to certain number of tries	Large organizations	Custom pricing. Plans are unlimited interviews. Per demo: Relationships start at $5,000/year
Competitor	One-way and live video interviewing; interview collaboration; interview scheduling	Claim: already has 3,000+ clients	Staffing companies, schools and small business	$99 (Bronze); $209 (Silver); $1,999 (Platinum). All plans unlimited interviews
Competitor	Video pitch; one way and live video interviewing	Promote easy-to-use interface Headquartered in the Netherlands	Large organizations such as ABC Recruiting and partnerships with businesses like BizExample	Custom pricing, All plans are unlimited interviews
Competitor	One way and live interviewing, Interview prep tool	Claim: already has 900+ clients	Mid-size & large organizations	Custom pricing
Competitor	One-way and live video interviewing	Offer interview analytics (HR team)	Mid-size & large organizations	$500/month (Basic); $950/month (Professional); $1,500/month (Corporate)
Competitor	One-way video interviewing	Candidates cannot erase, re-record	Headquartered in Paris with focus on European market	Purchase credits by number of positions or by number of interviews
Competitor	One way and live video interviewing	Text and audio options	Smaller businesses	Starting at $99 (Silver); $2,029 (Gold); Enterprise (call)
Competitor	One-way plus ATS system			295 /month (2 months cancellation notice)

They not only listed competitors but also went above and beyond. Mark considered what competitor services felt like from a consumer perspective. He tested their products and engaged their customer service. He knew their pricing and their features as well as their target audiences. Most importantly, his research was relatively unbiased. There was no hiding of good features or embellishing of bad features. No, Mark was honest with himself about who was in the market and how well they were performing. The competitor table for HelloCecil was so detailed that it was the only competitor analysis I didn't need to touch. Mark's work on it was perfect.

Don't Get Stuck: How to Get Started

To start on your Competitive Analysis, you may find it most helpful to start with a handwritten list. Brainstorm on what competitors you know of right off the top of your head. Add some extra notes about each competitor. What do you know to be true of each of them? From there, you can validate each fact by doing light research online. Then add your solid, verified facts to your main business plan.

As you wrap up this section, remember that you will want to revisit it in the future to make sure it is kept up-to-date. That is an important strategy to incorporate into your business activities. It only takes a few minutes to validate that your competitor table and takeaways are still accurate, which can help you stay in tune with your market.

The next part of this book will review the Market Entry section for your business plan. The Market Entry chapter is where you will take all you have learned about your industry and competitors and create an entrance plan based on data, research, and facts about the market. This is a pivot point where you are no longer researching and analyzing. You are focusing on the action steps to launch your business.

My Competitive Analysis includes:
- ❑ A list of what I already know about my top competitors
- ❑ A table with the information I researched about each known top competitor
- ❑ Addition of one to three competitors I did not consider or know about

Chapter 6

Market Entry Strategy

In the beginning, we started out using recycled bottles and filling them with our product in our garage, we were so small-time. We moved from that to ordering semi-trucks of bottles to fill an order. Looking at it that way, it helps us to appreciate how far we've come.

—Travis Rypkema and Josh Brazier,
co-founders of TNB Naturals

www.tnbnaturals.com

The very first e-mail I received from Travis read, "We have one of the largest distribution networks in the hydroponic industry." That kind of claim isn't a small one, so I was deeply intrigued with this business from the start. At the time, my work with them was focused on clarifying their business pitch and strategy for investor attraction. As I heard about their company and their launch, I was amazed at their back story.

TNB Naturals's flagship product is a natural CO_2 enhancer developed by Travis in his garage several years ago. Originally, the product was made to help his own plants grow by increasing CO_2 exposure. He quietly developed this when he realized other products available didn't create the best results. He created an all-natural, 100-percent-sustainable product that allows photosynthesis to occur more efficiently.

When his plants began growing exponentially more quickly and becoming more healthy, it marked the beginning of TNB Naturals. Through diligence, hard work, and a great partnership with Josh, who had been a friend of mine since high school days, the business began to grow steadily as a result of the founders' focused efforts. Six years later, TNB products are sold in more than 20 countries and are available in thousands of stores around the world. The company's lean structure allows them to stay operationally involved day-to-day, and they personally handle customer inquiries and focus heavily on giving back to their community.

Now that their business was growing and scaling, they wanted to carefully expand their product line. With newfound clarity on how the industry operated and the potential it bore, they realized they would have to grow further into the market very strategically. They needed the right amount of cash in order to make their growth dreams a reality, and they decided that an investor would be the right way to move forward.

When they contacted me to help develop their investor pitch, I knew they would instantly stand out to investors. It's not that they had flawlessly moved forward or avoided mistakes along the way—quite the contrary. Instead, they were going to stand out because of their positive attitude and self-awareness. Both Travis and Josh have admirable humility and a drive that is unstoppable. Built into their strategy is a goal-oriented approach in which they focus on the *what* and then back into the *how*. This simply isn't natural for most people.

Have you ever been in a position where you had a really good idea but didn't know how you would possibly get started? Maybe you decided you wanted to start a project but didn't quite know the right next step. Or maybe you contemplated moving homes or switching jobs but weren't quite sure where to start searching. These are times when you naturally get lost in the *how* step. It is a very human thing to do. So when Travis and Josh clearly approached things from a different perspective, it was really powerful to witness. And based on their success, their approach was clearly working.

The absolute biggest struggle for most entrepreneurs is developing the baby steps of how to start their business. Developing the Market Entry Strategy section can be hard if your goal isn't crystal clear in your mind. Once you know your goal, you can back into how to achieve that goal.

Let Me Be Honest with You

Building a business is like putting together a 1,000-piece puzzle without the picture to guide you. It isn't impossible to do, but it does require some visualizing and strategy to get it done. You have to avoid getting overwhelmed by all the little steps and unknown parts of the picture while still keeping the end goal in mind. Start with smaller goals such as finding the corners and edges and grouping the pieces of similar color. Before you know it, those small steps will add up, and your end goal—a finished picture—will come to life.

In the end, Travis and Josh shared some of their strategy and mindset tips with me. They had a shared vision board where they would write the next goal and give it their focus. Sometimes small, sometimes large, those goals started becoming accomplishments one at a time. They stayed diligent and positive, and after a while, all of those small goals led them to the moment when they realized they had created a company with global reach and huge potential. That was a long way to come from their days in the garage.

The Goal of Your Market Entry Strategy

Your Market Entry Strategy is the place in your business plan where you define your next goals for the immediate future. You will also map the early steps you will need to take in order to meet the goal set you laid out. That may sound a bit elementary, but this strategy segment is the pivotal point that leads so many businesses to failure. If you aren't clear and careful about the goals you set in this section, the rest of your business strategy will be unclear.

Travis and Josh had a clear goal. They wanted to launch an expansion to their product line, tap into the commercial product market, and distribute in 200 countries. They backed into their *how* strategy to reach these goals and realized they needed land and more space for their upcoming capacity needs. They determined which specific trade shows and expos would be valuable to attend in order to foster key relationships with new distributors and industry players, which would help them get closer to that 200 mark. They filled in a few other unknowns on how to move from their current state to their new goal. They backed into their entire business strategy by having a clear vision, which is what you will now do for your own business.

Impact of This Section for Investors

The Market Entry Strategy portion of your business plan will show investors how much redirecting you may or may not need to do. They will review this section for areas where you may show you are a bit inexperienced in how to make the right decisions, or where you may be working toward a goal the hard way. Investors are often open-minded here, looking for where their own expertise may bring value or whether your entry strategy is showing that you have a clear understanding of what the business needs to do to start strong.

When I worked on the investor pitch for TNB Naturals, I aimed to incorporate evidence of experience. Their ideal investor would see that these guys didn't need a boss to take over or motivate them; they were already driven and motivated. However, if the investor had advice to offer, Travis and Josh would certainly listen. Travis and Josh had a strategy that was carefully tied to the end goal(s) and based on what they knew could be highly effective. Through trial and error, they knew firsthand which conferences and expos to attend. They learned how to spark cold conversations with distributors and knew how to approach new information and unknown market segments with a learning mentality and willingness to pivot. This had to be clear in their pitch. They knew their goals, had a clear strategy, and would be the ideal entrepreneurs for busy investors to partner with.

Impact of This Section for Bankers

Your business bankers and underwriters are likely to apply common sense logic to this section. After all, they aren't experts in your business, so they may not be able to recognize whether your entry strategy is effective. Instead, they will be checking to make sure it seems practical and is understandable. For these reasons, you need to approach this section from a layperson's perspective and be sure to avoid heavy industry jargon, acronyms, or phrases that may lose your reviewer. Your audience should be able to come away thinking, "Okay, that seems to make sense."

Impact of This Section for Strategy

You will build your Market Entry Strategy to clearly depict your success plan for launch. If you are an existing business, this section will focus on the beginning of the next phase for your company. You will need to be careful to think through things at a level you can easily follow. This is where you can be as specific and detailed as you need to be in order to make this section impactful for you as you move forward. In some business plans I've supported where clarifying strategy was the goal, the end format was more of a checklist than a written chapter. You will still get layout advice at the end of this chapter, but know that I encourage you to take full liberty and design this section in the way that feels right for you.

Up until this point, the business plan has not been about your business. It has been a small feasibility study that leads your business to a clear goal and deliverables for your customers. Sometimes, the research chapters create a shift in focus, and sometimes they validate an existing focus. But either way, it's important to tackle market entry ahead of market entry. This is so you can let the research determine the right path.

Creating Your Market Entry Strategy

Your Market Entry Strategy will start with your goals. You will focus on key areas of your business and set goals for those areas. This chapter will offer the key areas that require goals and walk you through how to set goals for each area. Finally, you will be shown a simple way to finish your Market Entry Strategy by leveraging other parts you've completed thus far in your business plan.

Write the Industry Problem Statement

Here you will write the problem statement. This statement will be the drive behind your business goals. The competitor research you conducted in the last chapter will give you a clear gap to fill. You will take where the competition is failing miserably, take that away from what they do phenomenally, and marry that with what your industry is desperate for. Focus on the solution your business will bring to the market based on industry research and the competitive landscape.

To do this, list the overarching problem statement you plan to fix with your business. Here are some prompts that may help get you started:

> Right now, there are no providers who **offer a dry-cleaning pick-up and delivery service within 30 miles**.
> Customers are frustrated with local **daycare** options because **they aren't open after 5:00 p.m.**
> The biggest problem with **buying cars** is **dealing with sales-people**.
> Buyers wish **pajamas** were **more versatile for home office use**.

Once you have a problem statement, move on to how that problem can best be solved with your business solution.

Write the Solution Statement

Your solution statement comes next in your Market Entry Strategy. It should solve the problem directly and succinctly. It should tie in as if writing this business plan led you to this business idea, not vice versa. It will be a statement that serves as a focus and purpose for your business. To continue the example, the solution statements that align with the problem statements may be as follows:

> [Business name] will be the only dry cleaner offering pickup and delivery service within a three-town area.
>
> [Business name] will launch with extended daycare hours, operating from 7:00 a.m. to 7:00 p.m.
>
> [Business name] will enter the market as a disruptor by having digitized salesperson-less car transactions.
>
> [Business name] will launch a new pajama line that is casual and comfortable but looks suitable enough to be seen by colleagues during virtual meetings.

Now that you have simply stated the solution, it is time to explain your method of execution.

Explain the High-Level How

As you might guess, the next paragraph you will write will talk through *how* you plan to deliver your solution at a very high level. Sometimes, this step takes additional research, depending on your level of familiarity with your business direction. Or, if you have a partner, you may need to lean on each other's expertise to fill in the gaps.

For Travis and Josh of TNB Naturals, they balanced their knowledge sets well. Travis had never run a business before. He was happy to create new products but wasn't sure early on how to sell what he created. Josh, on the other hand, was an experienced entrepreneur. He had some understanding of how to start getting their product into stores.

If you are like Travis and feel like you may not know what you may not know, understand that this is a natural thing for everyone at the beginning. Start to combat the unknowns by moving into the discovery mindset. By this point, you've researched a ton about the industry and about your competitors, so you can continue the process by researching more about areas where you need more knowledge.

For instance, if you have a new product that you want to move into stores but don't know where to start, I recommend that you research that exact question: How do I get a new product into stores? The answers you will find online are often enough to get an idea of the general steps involved. Armed with general, public knowledge, you should be able to get started with your high-level *how* questions. No matter your business or industry, you will want to identify launch goals such as the following:

- How will you launch? Online, in a physical store, or a mix of both?
  - Why this strategy?
- How will your business begin on day 1? Go live all at once, or does it have components or revenue streams that will be phased in over time?
  - Why this approach?
- How will your business market to new customers about launch and grand open?
  - Why those mediums and methods?
- How will you make your business differentiator clear to each first customer?
  - Why is that an effective approach?

Answer these *how* questions from a bird's-eye view. They will help you focus on the right details in the next chapter when you work through your Operations section. For now, try not to get overwhelmed by details.

Now that you have your problem, solution, and high-level understanding of how you view those early days of your new business, you can pivot to your goals for customer perception.

Goals for Customer Perception

Customer perception is related to your brand and reputation. What are some of the things you want your business to be known for? That should be related more to your values and mission than to your actual product or service. While there are likely several great things you hope to be known for, whittle them down to four at the most.

You may also want to separate them into short-term and long-term goals. For example, your short-term goals may be related to establishing yourself as the fresh, new option for customers, but your long-term goals may be to establish a reputation for being an honest brand that routinely gives back to the community.

If you feel stuck on your goals for customer perception, consider a speedy brainstorming session. Set a timer for two minutes. During that time, try to write down all the words or phrases you would want your customers to write about you in future reviews. Some examples are things like "great quality," "fast delivery," or "friendly staff." Write whatever comes to mind without filtering or judging your thoughts. Then let an hour (or more) go by and do it again, aiming to generate new or different phrases. Now you should have a decent list of qualities or traits you want your brand to be associated with, and you can list them in your business plan.

This goal set is related to the unique deliverable or experience your company will provide, the product, service, or solution. Establish one to three unique differentiators for your offering and refer back to your market research. There is one thing your company will provide that is different than your competitors. There is one market segment that will most appreciate what your company provides.

Creating Your 5-P Plan for Relevance

Most new businesses are unaware of the latest shifts away from traditional marketing. Perhaps you have heard of the four Ps of marketing: product, price, place, and promotion. However, your market entry strategy needs to focus on strategies for the new era for businesses: the Era of Relevance. The *Harvard Business Review* published a great piece on this, defining the new landscape that will lead you to what it means to be successful in this new world of business. Excerpted from the *Harvard Business Review*, the five new Ps are the following:

1. Purpose: Customers feel the company shares and advances their values.
2. Pride: Customers feel proud and inspired to use the company's products and services.
3. Partnership: Customers feel the company relates to and works well with them.
4. Protection: Customers feel secure when doing business with the company.
5. Personalization: Customers feel their experiences with the company are continuously tailored to their needs and priorities.[7]

As you consider these five Ps for your business plan, think about one or two ways customers will perceive the relevance of your business in each area. Allow these prompts to help with direction on how to identify your relevance factor for customers in each area.

Purpose:
- Does your company feel strongly about preserving the environment?
- Does your company highly value individuality and self-acceptance?
- Does your company believe in giving to charity?

---

7. John Zealley, Robert Wollan, and Joshua Bellin, "Marketers Need to Stop Focusing on Loyalty and Start Thinking about Relevance," *Harvard Business Review* (March 21, 2018), https://hbr.org/2018/03/marketers-need-to-stop-focusing-on-loyalty-and-start-thinking-about-relevance.

Pride:

- Does your product or service make buyers feel like they are making a good ethical decision?
- Does the purchase of your product or service help someone or something in a unique way?
- Does your company have a way of influencing positive self-esteem or validation of self in some way?

Partnership:

- Does your buying process allow the buyer to make choices or have an element of control over the process?
- Do your customers have a way to directly interact with someone from your company at various stages of their relationship with your business?
- Is there an element of "we're in this together" at one or multiple stages of the customer journey?

Protection:

- Will you have text at your checkout point—either in-store or online—where you state your priority of safe transactions?
- Do you offer a clear and stress-free return, exchange, and refund policy?
- Will your customers expect to be treated as valuable persons who will not be judged and will be treated with dignity and respect?

Personalization:

- Is there a way you connect personally in-store with each buyer who comes in?
- Does your website have personalized shopping cart options where the customer might be addressed by name?
- Does your product or service come with a personal or unexpected gift, note, or other emotionally impactful bonus?

Your answers to the five Ps will be helpful in the next chapter when you organize your operational strategy based on these points and your overall goals outlined in this chapter.

Things to Avoid

You may find you have a new window of clarity in this section as your goals become clearer and the details begin to be tangible for you to envision. Try to avoid getting too detailed as you map out how you might reach these goals. If needed, you can even use bullets to help you maintain brevity in this chapter. You will get more detailed and more technical in the Operations section, so try to keep that in mind as you work through your goals.

Also, try to keep your goals focused on one general theme or idea. All goals listed here should support your immediate next phases in business, not market domination. There are a lot of entrepreneurs who have big visions of their idea being the next best thing. Whether you think your business could have a viral effect or could dominate a space, you need to remember as a start-up that your path to that point will likely take careful execution. Try to be mindful of your goals and make sure they are near-term targets that you hope to attain within the next few months up to the next three years. You can generally have bigger goals beyond that, of course—after all, it never helps to dream small! Just make sure your business plan content focuses more on the goals you most want to meet in the immediate future. These are your focus when it comes to market entry.

Technical Layout

Completing your market entry strategy should be more highlight-oriented than detailed execution plan. As mentioned, if it helps, you might go with bulleted lists or very short paragraphs as your chosen format for this section. That will help you stay concise with your goals.

Open with your differentiators and follow up with your *how* goals. Then be sure to explain how you plan to address your five Ps, which may take up a full page depending on how many ways you plan to address each point.

Market Entry Strategy

Pajama Business LLC

Buyers wish pajamas were more versatile for home office use. Pajama Business LLC will launch a new pajama line that has pajamas that are casual and comfortable but look suitable enough to be seen by colleagues during virtual meetings. Th business will launch online to start. This will allow for a low overhead structure, and larger profit margins for a faster breakeven point. After the business is profitable; a brick and mortar establishment will be added in Phase 3.

The product line will consist of pajama sets and individual tops and bottoms. Once this flagship product line is refined and achieves low return rates and high retention and referral rates, then the business will introduce slippers and robes. This will ensure the business is known for one core product – versatile pajamas – before broadening to other loungewear items.

The business will focus on an Instagram advertising strategy. Instagram has the highest value per sale at $65, compared to Facebook at $55 and YouTube at $37 (Hatch, 2018). This is a strong area for our team because of the co-founder's connection with an experienced Instagram influencer.

The problem message with current pajamas will also be better conveyed with the visual medium of Instagram, though we will work with other social and content means to connect with customers as well. Pajama Business LLC has a clear business differentiator that is better explained with photo or video, where we can demonstrate the problem better than solely explaining in words.

We want our customers to perceive our brand as reliable in customer service, high quality in fabric, and business-casual in style. We will be the unique solution for adults wanting a mix of comfort and style, with a mid-tier price tag.

Our Five P's of Relevance:

Purpose: Buyers are aligned to the business purpose, which is to maximize lifestyle freedom for each customer.

Pride: Buyers will feel proud to wear this select clothing line, catered to home-based professionals and designated to serve independent-minded professionals, and designated to serve independent minded professionals and entrepreneurs who value their time and think innovatively.

Partnership: With a try-it-first program and a human-based customer service system, customers will feel they are heard and that their satisfaction matters to us as much as it does to them.

Protection: Buyers will make purchases on our SSL-encrypted site, and a no-frills return and exchange policy will make any purchase one that is worry-free.

Personalization: Customers will be given a surprise gift with each purchase: a mug, sleep mask, or stress ball to add an extra "thanks" for every purchase.

Figure 2: Mugs will be purchased in bulk and personalized with five different phrases. A mug is one of the free gifts with each purchase.

Finishing the TNB Naturals Business Pitch

TNB Naturals took a highly strategic entry path with zero funding and grew to a multi-million-dollar, multinational business. The founders were focused on the next phase of their business, which was market entry of their product into more countries and expansion of their product line. They had a market entry strategy that included lessons learned from their bootstrapping efforts and had goals that were clear and attainable.

When developing the content for their investor pitch, I was focused on capturing the great successes they had achieved to date as well as mapping their market entry ambitions. For the owners, looking back

Market Entry Strategy

Our goal is to open new relationships with distributors in 200 countries. We are already well established in 25 countries. Through strategy, we have secured the biggest wholesalers in Canada, Spain, Africa, Russia, Turkey, the US, France, Australia, and the UK. We have diligently worked to create a distributor pipeline that increases access to hydroponic stores and other sellers globally. The distributors we are partnered with have helped us grow our credibility with other distributors, which is clear in new agreements we are actively pursuing.

We are primarily in the hydroponic industry and are actively looking to expand into new arenas. For instance, we recently signed a deal with Olympic snowboarding gold medalist Ross R., a growing entrepreneur and strong supporter of cannabis and associated products. He has agreed to include our products in his business product kits in places such as Canadian Tire and additional stores with garden centers stores, which will expand our products into new markets.

Our flagship product is an all-natural, 100-percent-sustainable CO2 enhancer that allows photosynthesis to occur more efficiently. Th This directly results in better crop yields. It has a long shelf life, is refillable, is safe, and is extremely easy to use. As a product that is "active" during the day and is less "active" without daylight, it is the only product on the market that mimics natural growing conditions for better crop health.

We see opportunity to expand further within the agriculture/hydroponics industry with additional products in R&D phase. With clarity on how to grow forward, we are excited to invite a silent investor to mutually benefit from our continuing growth.

Our First Phase of Market Entry

For the first years of existence, we have focused on building our business. Every distributor who has ordered from our product line has become a repeat buyer. This 100 percent retention rate has allowed us low acquisition costs and high return on every dollar. For that reason, we've had the liberty to reinvest profit dollars back into growing the business. From selling one bottle in our garage, we've grown this business into a multimillion-dollar company.

Figure 1 Above: Our original flagship product is now an international product. We aim to get this into 200 countries in the coming years.

was needed context in order to show forward goals. After all, securing distribution deals that would put them in 200 countries may sound far-fetched in isolation. However, investors needed to see what had already been done—just a very recent snapshot—so they could understand why this team could clearly envision such an aggressive market entry plan.

Don't Get Stuck: How to Get Started

You already know your problem statements based on the research you have done so far, and you likely understand how your product or service meets that need. Start with these known elements and jot down your problem and solution statements. These should be in the early part of your Market Entry chapter, not buried in the middle or bottom. Then you can move on to your goals and *how* statements.

If you feel like you can't envision your goals enough to start the *how* section, consider first listing your wants for your business. Think about it in terms of what would make you feel accomplished or successful by the end of year one. Is it a certain revenue goal? It is a personnel count? Is it a huge customer base or rave reviews from the industry? Use these starting points, these wants and visions, to back into your high-level *how* statements.

The next chapter will consider the operations needed to meet the goals you outline in this chapter. This is where you will work through your personnel needs, your marketing plan, and the elements you will need for your day-to-day business activities. The next section of your business plan will be both more detailed and a bit longer than the Market Entry section, so clear your mind and keep your momentum. Believe it or not, the hardest parts of your business plan are behind you!

My Market Entry Strategy includes:

- ❑ The Problem Statement for my industry
- ❑ My Solution Statement
- ❑ How my business will bring this to market
- ❑ My goals for customer perception
- ❑ My 5-P plan for relevance

Chapter 7

Operations

At this point, I'm sitting here realizing that I don't know what I don't know. This is going to be a pretty new type of business, and there will be lessons learned that I haven't thought about yet. It's not intimidating at all if you just know that there's some things that will be choppy and there will be things you don't know.

—Rob Harmon, founder of Water Elephant

www.waterelephant.com

Rob Harmon had painstakingly developed a well detailed, totally comprehensive business case on his own. His business, Water Elephant, is a start-up concept that is the first totally "healthier for you" convenience store in a brick-and-mortar location. In concept, it is akin to a simplified version of Whole Foods Market. The business brings convenience to healthy living by selling only non-artificial ingredient food and beverages instead of the typically unhealthy options available in traditional convenience stores. The business is still in concept phase, and Rob is working through fund-raising with his finished business plan. However, with Rob's strategy and the right amount of future investor support, this business could launch and become profitable much more quickly than the average start-up.

When Rob and I initially connected, Rob was in a great situation. He had drummed up early investor interest and then contacted me to help get his documents investor-ready. This wasn't Rob's first business endeavor, but he spoke about it like it would become his magnum opus. This was a business he cared about personally and passionately. His drive and interest in seeing this concept succeed motivated me deeply, too.

When Rob first contacted me, he was trying to maximize his odds to secure an investor and had a specific deadline in mind to pitch his opportunity. Like most revision projects I take on, I knew there was going to be a lot of time and effort needed to reposition some concepts, weave in some new components, and create a nice flow for how the business plan would be presented. One area that completely floored me was his operations plan. He had a strategy that was thorough and detailed, covering nuances that only an experienced business owner would think about. I wondered if I would be able to add any extra value to that section of his plan.

My goal for his business plan was to make sure investors understood the concept and why it was unique. I also needed to explain how deep his experience was. He was raised in an entrepreneurial family, had started his own fitness business, and had ample leadership experience in corporate America. His knowledge was specific on how to manage restaurants, food and beverage stores, and convenience markets. He knew how to position things to sell, knew what people wanted to buy, knew the intricacies of creating a positive environment for happy employees, and knew how to manage a well oiled supply chain. He not only was brilliant in his understanding of his new business and market, but he was humbly focused on bringing health and happiness to his community by launching this store.

Usually when I hear about the operations side of a business concept, I immediately can pick out what needs to be added, validated by data, or changed. With Rob, no red flags jumped out at me. He had already researched his target audience, his market, the industry trends, and his competitors very thoroughly, and he used all of that to develop a robust operations plan. He also knew his price points, the best store layout, and granular things such as how social media was going to be used and the features of his ideal location. It was extremely impressive.

Have you ever seen one of those 3-D pictures that have hidden images in them? They look like an abstract drawing or painting at first, but when you adjust your focus, you can see a whole new aspect of the picture pop out at you. I saw one in a waiting room once, or so I thought. After several minutes of staring at a framed picture on the wall, trying to find the hidden 3-D image, I asked the receptionist what the hidden image looked like because I couldn't find it. She patiently informed me that there was nothing there to find. It was just an abstract drawing and not one of those eye-trick pictures.

Rob's plan was like that picture. I was looking for something that wasn't there. I spent more time than I'd like to admit trying to find holes to fill, specifically in Rob's Operations plan. In the end, I realized that he had done a really complete job, and there was no gap or omission to find or fix. He nailed it! What I needed to focus on was making sure it was beautifully and clearly presented.

Let Me Be Honest with You

Your Operations plan is your best attempt at mapping out the day-to-day life of your business. Even if you have your map perfectly in your mind, you might find it really hard to show it just as perfectly on paper. A confusing, jumbled, or poorly formatted Operations section will be a detriment to your business plan. This section needs to be very organized and feel like a small instruction manual for how to run the business you have in mind.

In the end, I did heavy formatting on Rob's business plan, and the Operations section received special attention. His ideal inventory selection, his growth plan and scale goals, and his employee and training expectations were all displayed carefully and with visuals where possible. The final product had a very intentional flow and tone and highlighted Rob's clear understanding of his future business model.

The Goal of Your Operations Section

The Operations section of your business plan is meant to reveal the path from what is in your mind to what will happen in reality. Your day-to-day operations may have been clear as day in your head up to this point, but now you will put it on paper and work through whether your vision needs a bit more detail added. You should expect that you change some core concepts or add new elements as you think things through in more detail as a natural part of the process.

When I worked through Rob's business plan, his perfect operations plan was unexpected. I'd never seen one so thoroughly done at this stage in the business plan development before, and it took a while to accept that it didn't need to be changed. However, looking back, it makes sense. He has direct experience in the industry. He's lived and breathed this business for a long time and had ironed out the details a while ago. Rob knew exactly what he was doing.

Impact of This Section for Investors

Investors will look at this section to see if you are able to translate a great idea into an actionable plan. Are you solely a dreamer with grand ideas but no ability to take steps toward making it reality? Or are you able to dream big and then work through the steps needed to make the dream become your reality? The investor will likely see areas to be updated, changed, or added based on his or her own experience, and that's okay. This section is less about right and wrong and more about your willingness and ability to create a more granular, practical look at executing your vision.

Rob's business plan had an Operations section that had great detail and very rounded information. He knew so much, in fact, that a stranger could have picked up his business plan and largely launched the business with no further explanation needed. Most businesses don't have this level of depth in their plan, and not all businesses need this level of depth; but for Rob, it was a great way to showcase his strengths as an owner to investors.

Impact of This Section for Bankers

Your underwriting team will look for whether you have truly thought all of this through from a leader perspective. You think you have a great business concept, but are you viewing it like an owner? Are you accurately planning out the way you will run your business and how your daily operations will flow? Your ability to explain the daily operations on paper shows that you are grounded in your vision and that you have a clear way to make it succeed.

Impact of This Section for Strategy

When you begin building your Operations section, you will be doing the most important thing that every business owner does: turning thoughts into action. Your Operations section will force you to think about the daily grind of running your business and what you might need to do to make it optimal. Here, a T-shirt business might begin to realize that a huge staff is needed to operate the company day-to-day. Or a restaurant could realize that its online marketing strategy will need serious focus and investment, more than originally thought. A pet sitting business may realize that there are several permits and licenses needed before it can start operating. There should be new levels of clarity as you work through this section, and getting to this clarity now will increase your odds for success later.

Creating Your Operations Section

The Operations section will be a build of several smaller components. Depending on your business, you may have more subsections than shown in this chapter. You will want to add subheadings as needed to capture all the nuances of your business. Here, I will review the must-haves so you can prepare for the bare minimum list of sections to include in your Operations section.

Licenses and Permits

If your business accepts payments from customers, then it will need to be legally structured to do so. That means you need to make sure your business entity is registered and ready to begin tracking and reporting generated income. I know this is not fun and can even seem daunting at first. However, I promise you will get through it if you try. Many sites that provide information on this can feel clunky or be hard to navigate, especially if run by a local government. If you can overlook any lack of user-friendliness, you will find that most license and permit applications are pretty straightforward and simple to complete and submit.

Every state, city, and county may have their own business requirements. Usually they are inexpensive and simple to file, although some may take longer to receive approval from than others. Some common types of licenses include the following:

Common State Requirements
- General Business License
- Sales Tax Permit
- Doing Business As (DBA) License

Common Local (County, City) Requirements
- Zoning Permit
- Home Occupation Permit
- Heath and Food Handling Permit
- Building and Fire Code Permits
- Environmental and Pollution Licenses and Permits
- Signage Permits

You need to research your business's requirements based on your business structure and where your entity is registered. The type of business you have will also impact what types of licenses or permits you need. For example, a car wash has different legal obligations to the county and city than a restaurant. An e-commerce site operator has different sales tax obligations than a virtual assistant staffing business. You need to make yourself aware of your obligations based on your business, your location, and your activities.

Many of these requirements also include a renewal stipulation. That means you may need to renew a license or permit every quarter or every year or two, or even reapply upon an expiration period. Other requirements are one-time filings that you only need to handle at the very start of your business. Make a list of what you need to apply for and add it to your Operations section. After you have clarity on how to legally operate in compliance, you can move on to who you will need on your team in order to begin functioning as a business.

In-House Team

Your team will change over time, and your job in this subsection is to identify the day-one team members you will need on staff or under contract in order to open your business. Try not to over-think this; it's okay if you have a small team to start. This section can always be updated later, and you can begin by listing positions that immediately come to mind. Will you need a salesperson? A financial person? Will you hire support people, legal experts, or social media managers? Think about who you will need in-house to help you start your business.

To show them clearly, add an organization chart listing each position in your new company. If you already know who each person will be, feel free to add their names. As you think through the title for each position, remember that your salary needs for your budget will be tied to how you label your team members. A customer service associate has a different salary range than a retail sales representative. Do a quick search on each title and read the associated job descriptions. Make sure you are targeting the right type of role, and then make note of the salary range for each position. You will need this information handy soon for your financial projections.

Once you have a simple organization chart with core team members, add a brief couple of sentences on what each role will entail and why you need them on board. List what each position will do to support the business. If you know who you will hire for a role, add their name and explain why they would be perfect as an employee for your company.

Outsourced Team

You may be thinking that some roles will be filled by people you decide not to have on payroll as employees. This is common for start-ups and is usually a huge money-saving decision. Think about the needs you will have in your business. Are any of those needs easy to fill by contracted or remote workers? Here are some common positions that start-ups tend to outsource:

- Bookkeeping and accounting
- Customer service support
- Website development and SEO support
- Blog, social media, e-mail content creation
- IT support
- Payroll services
- Human resources and hiring support
- Marketing activities

If you take a moment to think through the things you may not want to handle every day as a business owner, you may find that some tasks are simple or monotonous enough to outsource. Being the do-it-all business owner may seem like an easy way to save on costs in the short term. And for your business, you may be absolutely right. However, in the long term as your business grows, you will need to see clearly where your business needs outside support. You might have the most clarity on those areas of need now, before you ever approach the point of being overwhelmed by daily business activities.

To project where you might hire an outsourced team, take time to consider the following:

- Where am I really uncomfortable? What problems would be outside my skill set?
  Examples: Technical problems, marketing problems, personnel problems, writing needs, finances and money management, customer service.
- Can I afford to spend time troubleshooting or researching a solution or learning a new skill to close this gap?
- Would this problem come up often enough to justify hiring a full-time employee to handle it?

If you have clear areas where you can see yourself getting stuck executing solutions for problems that are outside your comfort zone, and if you have no time or desire to gain more mastery in that area, then you need to prepare for help now. If that area is a core part of your business, one that will likely require full-time support indefinitely, then consider adding that role to your organization chart. Otherwise, you may be better off outsourcing that job to a contracted person or company who can handle that one task or area of need.

List the positions you may want to outsource later. Add those roles in bullet form and explain briefly the specific ways each position will support the business. Also, note why a full-time staff member wouldn't be preferred. That may be because you are aiming for cost savings, opting for short-term support, or seeking to work with an expert provider who specializes in the area of need.

Now that you understand how your team will look, it's time to understand how you will attract clients to your business through marketing efforts.

Marketing

In this subsection, you will list your core methods of marketing and why those are ideal. These methods should take your competitors into consideration. Are you copying what others are doing to attract clients?

Or are you using a unique strategy? Below are some common areas start-ups focus on for customer acquisition:

- Visual social media
    - Facebook
    - YouTube
    - Instagram
- Written forum content
    - Reddit
    - Blogs
    - Ezine articles
- Live events
    - Conferences
    - Trade shows
    - Networking events
- Traditional media
    - Radio
    - TV
    - Newspaper
    - Mailers and flyers
    - Billboards

Online Strategy Considerations

Your online strategy will have a role in your business. If you aren't sure where to start with this, consider checking out the strategy your competition has adopted. One way to look at how your competition is getting online traffic and conducting online marketing is by using an online tool. Most tools are free, and if you simply search "competitor SEO," you will find plenty of tools available to check out how your competition gets their customers. My personal favorites are www.spyfu.com and www.similarweb.com, but there are plenty of options available beyond these. Consider the results and think through whether you want to mimic your competitor's strategies or tackle a whole new, untapped approach to reach your market.

You should know there are two schools of thought on this. One school says you *should* copy your competitor's strategies because they are using what seems to work for the target market. It's as if they already found the best option that generates great results, so you can simply copy this proven method. With this approach, you need to know that you will be joining a sea of competitors, so it may be harder to stand out.

The other school of thought says that you should look where no other competitor is advertising and use that method. This line of thinking says that you will have an easier access point to your audience if you aren't competing for their attention alongside your own competitors. With this approach, you need to know that the competition may not be advertising a specific way for a reason. They may have tried it already and found that their customers just don't respond well to that method or medium of marketing.

No matter which route you go, definitely address whether you will market entirely online, in print or through traditional media, or a hybrid of approaches. You want to answer these questions now before creating the budget for your marketing needs. That way, you will be more likely to create a budget that makes sense for your business.

And remember, this may also be an area you need to outsource. Online strategy is very important, and if it isn't your area of expertise, it is okay to outsource it. I personally recommend providers who are really skilled in supporting start-ups, like www.Ambition.Agency that does everything from helping with your marketing strategy to website development to logo and branding support. Such providers can help you define your business messaging early on, which can help your business become more established much faster.

Once your marketing vision is documented, you can think through what a grand open will look like for your new business.

Grand Open Event

Your grand open activities relate to the day you open your doors and (hopefully!) greet your first batch of eager customers. For online businesses, this is called "launching" when you may create a ton of blog posts, advertisements, and general awareness around your upcoming grand open day. Perhaps on this day, all customers get a free gift or special discount. The grand open is treated as a very special event and is aimed at starting the business on a very lucrative note by generating buzz.

For brick-and-mortar stores, the concept is the same and may have the same activities that an online launch would have. Your business will want to spread the word locally that your business opens soon, and on the grand open day, there will be special events, giveaways, or incentives to encourage new customers to stop by for a visit.

If your business will have a phased grand open, it's okay to have a main grand open and a grand reopen in the next phase. This is common for more complex businesses that have unique revenue streams they cannot start all at the same time. Rob did this with Water Elephant. There will be a piece of his business in the future called the "lab store" that will include food preparation activities. That piece of the business will experience its own grand open event. Each major part of the business receives its own strong start as the business grows and expands.

Daily Activities

Your daily activities are where you can paint the picture of how your business will operate. From the navigation of your customers, to the hours you will be open, to the way you plan to collect payments, to whether your employees will wear name tags—this is where you can talk through your details.

As you consider this, consider a day in the life of your business about a month after you open. Think through a slow day and a busy day and how each may look.

Unless you have already run a similar business, know that you will be guessing quite a bit here. And that's okay. There is a lot that you simply cannot know until you start operating. Try not to let that intimidate you. In fact, you probably know more than you give yourself credit for at this point. Just jot down a day in the life and see what unfolds. If you feel like you have big gaps, consider interviewing a business owner who is in a similar space. It doesn't have to be a competitor or even the same kind of business. Just find someone close enough to have overlap in the business you are trying to create. Or check out online business owner forums and post some open-ended questions such as the following:

- What operations challenges were you unprepared for when you started your business?
- What operational mistakes cost you the most money when you first started?
- What did you think was true about your business needs when you first launched, and which ones turned out to be totally wrong?

Posting these types of questions publicly or privately in specific social media groups and pages and seeing what answers you get can be very enlightening. I could help you close some gaps in your operational plan.

Things to Avoid

Try to avoid developing your complete operations manual and handbook in the body of your business plan. As you work through the Operations section of your business plan, you may find that there is a *lot* of ground to cover. Keep in mind that you may want to place the bulk of a subsection into your Appendix. If a subsection runs more than one page, that may be a sign that the content should be abbreviated for your Operations chapter and the extra detail added to the Appendix section of your business plan.

For some business types, it can be natural to end up with a very comprehensive output that shows a granular level of detail for your daily business operations. In your Operations section, it's okay to touch on things like operating hours, some high-level employee policies, or customer service goals, but avoid listing entire HR policies or creating a true process document in the main plan. You can plan to create those and make them action items, but do not actually create them in your business plan unless they are placed in the Appendix.

Technical Layout

Your Operations section will include an organization chart and will likely have more bulleted lists, side comments, and even tables than your other sections. If your business has processes that overlap or are closely related, consider adding a Gantt chart or visual depiction to map out any parts of the process that are interdependent.

The Operations section will have several short subsections outlining the various aspects of your daily operations and launch plans. Try to make sure that your Operations section takes up no more than one-fourth of your entire business plan. That means if your business

Operations

Pajama Business LLC

Team

Operations Manager Tammy Jane will support with core activities for the business, including calling the Union Hall for union labor support and managing project fulfillment options from an office perspective. Additional team members will include a fulfillment manager, customer service manager, and vendor support. These members will be given union-based pay rates and will be the core team. Ramp up of additional skilled labor personnel will be required for orders that require more manpower.

Mary Smith
Co-Founder & PM

Tammy Jane, COO

Mike Smith,
Office Manager & PM

Support Person

Support Person

Support Person

Fulfillment – PO to Order Placement

The business owners, Mike Smith and Mary Jones, will act as project managers in the supply chain process for order fulfillment until the business is ready to outsource order and fulfillment.

	Duration	Phase 1	Phase 2	Phase 3	Phase 4	Phase 5
PO to MFG	1-2 hours					
Material Order	1-2 days					
Embroidery and Detail	4 hours					
Arrival: Other materials*	5-7 days					
Final buttons and sewing	3 hours					
Boxing & Ship	5 mins					

plan is 20 pages long, your Operations section should not be more than five pages. Any extra content should be placed—you guessed it—in the Appendix.

Finishing the Water Elephant Business Plan

When I supported the business plan for Water Elephant, formatting was the core focus. Rob's original draft was text-only and had good information, but it needed to be better developed visually. I wanted his Operations chapter to come to life and show how detailed and particular the vision was. I was careful to use his brand colors throughout as an aesthetic extra, and I used bullets and tables everywhere possible.

WATER ELEPHANT

Operations

Organization Chart: Store 1 Open

Rob Hamilton
General Manager & Store Manager

Outsourced Payroll / Bookkeeper · Outsourced IT · Outsourced Social Media · Key Employee # 1 Manager in Training · Key Employee # 2 Manager in Training · Shift Leader #1 · Shift Leader #2

The first Water Elephant Oasis will be in the Greater Austin, Texas area. Numerous sites have been explored while looking for the below characteristics.

Location
- Local - Greater Austin area
- High visibility - high traffic
- Good access / egress
- Building located near the street like a convenience store or QSR
- Hipsters, families, Hispanics, blue collar, local business buildings, manufacturing, schools, athletic fields and stadiums, etc. part of the consideration set
- Well lighted
- Favorable zoning - signage
- Lease agreement terms reasonable

Building
- Parking next to the curb
- Corner and drive-through capability is optimum
- Good visibility from parking lot to the inside of the store

Rob had wonderful concept images created, so I used those in the Operations chapter as well. That helped show and demonstrate the final vision for the store. At a glance, investors could see that the strategy had both depth and simplicity. It was skimmable yet comprehensive and very easy to understand.

Most importantly, the operational strategy was very realistic. It clearly showed how the store would open and operate, where it would be located, and what it would sell. It reviewed marketing goals and personnel plans. Rob did an excellent job with his vision, and that made it really exciting for me to make that vision "pop" on paper.

Don't Get Stuck: How to Get Started

If you feel like there are too many details to consider, you may want to start with imagining hour-by-hour what would happen in your live business. Think about starting your day. Would there be employees to call? Customers to service? Vendors to contact? What would be the next actions you would need to take by 10:00 a.m.? Use this moment to really tap into the moving parts of your business—the people, the money that will need to go in and out, the marketing, the customers, the hours. Start jotting down the details you are envisioning and begin categorizing them as "marketing" or "employees" and such, and begin from there.

Once you have worked through the details for your operations and grand open activities, it is time to put them into a schedule. There needs to be a clear timeline for the schedule of events leading up to your new business so you can stay on track and really map out how everything will fall into place. You will learn a quick way to develop a schedule in the next chapter.

My Operations Section includes:

- ❑ A list of needed licenses and permits
- ❑ A team organization chart
- ❑ A marketing plan
- ❑ A strategy for my business's online/digital presence
- ❑ My Grand Open plans
- ❑ A summary of daily activities for my business

Chapter 8

Schedule

This thing needs to live on beyond me, you know? It's a big project, it will take time. But if something happens to me before we launch, I need people I can trust. That's why I need good partners, like Edwin. To keep it going no matter what.

—Philip Agostini, co-founder of AmaZone New York
and AmaZone Sao Paulo

http://amazonenewyork.com

A M A Z O N E

THEME PARK
NEW YORK

"We want to build the world's largest indoor Amazon Rainforest replica on Earth." That was the opening line from two gentlemen, Philip Agostini and Edwin German, who asked me to write their business plan. Their next line was this: "We need to raise about $500 million to make it work." They explained how they knew their asking amount might be more or less than what they outlined and that they had already shifted their launch schedule several times up to this point.

This was one of those situations where I felt like it was destiny that we were in touch with each other. I had just been talking with my husband about how hard it is sometimes to communicate the need for a bigger asking amount or a shift in the projected schedule after working a business plan. Often, an entrepreneur comes to me with a ballpark in mind of how much money he or she needs to launch or how long it will take to get started. Sometimes, after building projections and clarifying the scope, I can see that a different amount of money is needed and that things will need to happen faster or slower than originally expected.

Unfortunately, some founders don't like to hear that. They aren't comfortable asking for more money or don't think they can execute their schedule faster than they planned. And that's okay if they want to stick with their original thoughts, but part of my job is to expose new angles that may not have been obvious to the entrepreneur in the beginning. Based on the initial conversation with Philip and Edwin, it seemed like they wanted the business plan and also some candid feedback on their assumptions.

When talking with these gentlemen, they described their vision to revitalize the Coney Island area of New York. Watching the historic amusement park over the decades made this duo realize that there was a death happening before their eyes—that the Coney Island area was in need of new life. They also knew that the local economy would see a huge awakening if they could create this indoor park. With Edwin's passion for supporting the economy in his home city and Philip's passion for rainforest preservation in his second home in Brazil, these lifelong friends teamed up to launch a new project. Both visionaries and highly successful in their own right, they had made this their side project over the course of 20 years.

So for them, building out a five-year schedule for when New York would get the world-renowned tourist attraction seemed like a short time away in the grand scheme of things. However, I remember wondering if they were overestimating this timeline. It crossed my mind that maybe they were even procrastinating a bit.

Have you ever talked to someone with great ambitions and vision who is always "about to do something great"? They seem to be extremely motivated to execute this awesome idea or new project or even a new business. However, when you get into details about when they plan to move forward, things seem to keep shifting. The timeline keeps getting moved for one reason or another, and after awhile, it just seems like they are procrastinating.

Heck, I've even been that person myself. There are always a slew of mini-projects I want to launch—writing a book, starting a micro business, enrolling in a program—and for one reason or another, I find myself pushing things out. I say to myself that the timing isn't right or there are other priorities to handle first. In those moments, others who can simply bring awareness to that pattern are essential for me. Sometimes, all I need is someone to tell me, "You've been saying you were working on that for a while now. Are you *really* doing it?"

I worried big-time about the timeline Philip and Edwin laid out for me. I needed to figure out a way to show how the business was launching fast enough. Meanwhile, I hoped Philip and Edwin were not extending the timeline forward unnecessarily. They had the original dream decades ago and in recent years had mapped out how they could execute their vision, and the next step was simply to take action. More importantly, that action had to be fast enough to attract investors who would want to see a quick return on their large investment. My challenge was to find out whether the timeline really made sense and whether I could articulate the timeline in a way that wouldn't put a damper on investor excitement.

Let Me Be Honest with You

Having an unrealistic schedule can be detrimental to your entire launch. It can lead to wasted time, missed opportunities, and general unpreparedness. An unrealistic schedule is like jumping on to an automated call and getting in line for the next available representative. When the automated system tells you that "someone will be with you shortly," you may find that you've wasted 30 minutes of your time simply waiting. After all, you don't want to hang up now; you may be next in line! However, if that system says, "You are number 31 in line, and someone will be with you shortly," you may decide you don't have time to wait.

This effect is the same with your business plan schedule. If you are building it for someone else—a partner, an investor, or a banker—then this is their indicator of whether they have time to watch the business hit certain milestones. If you are building it for yourself, then it will also be a gut check for you. Can you wait that long for the business to hit these milestones? If you plan to launch in a year, do you have the personal cash to sustain that long? If you plan to launch next month, is that really enough time to execute all the activities planned in your launch strategy?

In the end, I came to generally agree with Philip and Edwin's lengthy timeline. They were being conservative but were still within the realm of reality. They generally knew what they needed from the city, how funding rounds would work, and even how long construction plans would take in order for everything to come together properly. And all of these things would likely take a few years to execute properly. Still, the challenge of showing investors a project plan that would reveal immediate momentum was a present issue. I didn't want to deter investors who may see the project as too early to invest in, but I also couldn't risk being misleading about the timeline in any way.

The Goal of Your Schedule

This Schedule section is where you design your journey in the most concrete way possible. It is where the plan is least abstract. Clarity is key. This will serve as a timeline and action plan for the next months ahead. And above all, this is where you should aim to be as realistic as possible, not overly aggressive or conservative.

Importance of this Section for Investors

Investors will review this section to understand whether you have a schedule that fits their investment timing. If investors buy into your business too early, they have increased risk. The earlier your business idea, the more likely it will change in unpredictable ways.

When Philip and Edwin first envisioned this Coney Island amusement park, it wasn't an indoor Amazon preservation project at all. Instead, it was meant to be a water park. It was envisioned to be the only water park in the city, a place that would give residents and tourists an alternative to the beach during summer visits. Had investors come on board back then, they would have likely been shocked at the complete morph the project has taken since. They may have invested differently if they had known the business was headed in this direction. For this reason, investors see this section as their way to gauge whether the timing is right for their involvement.

Importance of this Section for Bankers

For bankers, your loan distribution and repayment plan will be gauged by the context of your schedule. If all spending activity happens at once, that tells a different story to underwriters than if your launch schedule occurs over the course of 18 months. It also shows whether the date of the grand open for your business is soon enough for their appetites. Some underwriters see a long-term launch plan and may have concerns that the revenue streams are starting too far in the future to be able to support the loan repayments for awhile. Or your schedule may seem unrealistically compressed, so you may appear to be missing critical steps. All of this goes into bankers' risk considerations.

Importance of This Section for Strategy

If you take a look at your schedule, it will force you to get honest about your next steps. Do you clearly understand what needs to happen over the course of the next year? Are you being realistic about each step in the process, or are you assuming a best or worst case scenario with each step?

Most importantly, when you step back and look at the entire timeline, you have to decide whether you can execute that timeline or whether you need to make other decisions. Maybe you realize that waiting six months for revenue to start is not something you can sustain, and perhaps you will get a part-time job to keep things afloat in the meantime. Maybe you see a milestone in your schedule that could derail other steps if delayed, and you decide to start that milestone earlier in your plan. Awareness of these variables is key to keeping you on the right track at the right pace.

Creating Your Schedule

Before we get started, you should know that there's no wrong detail to include in your schedule, and your dates will likely shift. It's rare for everything to hit its original milestone, and that's okay. Don't get stuck on the dates. Plug them in and try to work with them as real deadlines and adjust the deadlines if they pass.

Two Snapshot Views of Your Actions

The Schedule section of your business plan will be a snapshot of your actions in a quick, digestible format. Sometimes, it's appropriate to have two views of your schedule. In your business plan, you should show only the high-level, big-picture view. For your own purposes, you may have a more administrative view that you want to include. Both are important, so let's talk about the fastest way to compile each.

The Administrative View

You will have one schedule that will serve as a to-do list. This view will include any action items you may have jotted down as you built your business plan to this point. It may include things you need to do to start a brick-and-mortar business such as submitting permit requests to the city or listing job postings online. Your to-do list may include choosing a website provider or may have an action to launch a marketing campaign before grand open. No matter how complex or simple the action, be sure to add a deadline. The deadline can be a specific date, week, or month.

When you build this list, aim to stagger activities as much as possible. One rule of thumb is to avoid any gaps greater than two weeks. By having an action due every couple of weeks, you maintain momentum and avoid stagnating in your progress.

When the list is compiled, take a step back and look for steps that could easily cause delays or unexpected issues. With Edwin and Philip, their project launch was dependent on approval to use a certain plot of land near Coney Island. When I flew to New York to see the space, I agreed that it was the perfect location. If they can't build there, it would impact several areas of the business vision and require huge strategy shifts and a total timeline overhaul. They added action steps ahead of this land approval that would help maximize their odds for getting approval. They added "understand the bidding process for the land" and "find out who the point of contact is for the land bidding." With these added steps, they felt more prepared, felt they knew the micro steps to take to bring the best result, and clearly saw the pivot point for the next phase of their launch and were prepared for it, whichever way it would go.

Because the administrative schedule can be lengthy, it doesn't belong in the main section of your business plan. It belongs in the Appendix and should be easily accessible in editable form so you can keep it updated. If you are submitting this plan to anyone, make sure you include both open actions and actions completed to date, and do not delete or remove completed actions. That is how you will show your momentum and ability to manage all aspects of your business, even at an early stage.

The Big-Picture View

The big-picture schedule is what goes into the Schedule section of your business plan. It will be your quarterly schedule of goals, the big picture items you plan to accomplish in your business over the next four to five quarters. In the end, this will serve as a snapshot of what is represented in your administrative schedule.

Building this in snapshot view will be important to evaluate the real progress your business is making. It is also an introduction to a key best practice: quarterly business reviews when your business is live. By setting aside time every quarter to review the goals you set last quarter, you create an opportunity to evaluate things that need attention or goals that need to be adjusted.

This practice is essential even if your schedule spans years instead of quarters. For Philip and Edwin, I opted for a Gantt chart timeline that displayed years instead of a quarterly schedule. This was the most realistic and honest way to depict the plans for the project in a nutshell. Even still, Philip and Edwin visit regularly to strategize and collaborate on their progress and goals for the project and update their timeline as needed, both short term and long term.

The Schedule section of your business plan should show in a limited number of actions exactly how your business will proceed. It is something that comes later in your business plan as a result of everything you learn along the way in building your plan step-by-step. Even still, as you arrange your actions into a Schedule at this point, know that you may still have actions to add based on what you learn when you build out your financials.

Things to Avoid

When you are building your Schedule in your business plan, try to incorporate the goal of each action. Instead of just listing "get a website and web design provider," try this: "Establish online presence with a website and provider to help maximize traffic strategy." It will help you stay focused on the *why* for each action and will create clarity around your planning.

Another thing to avoid is getting too detailed in your big-picture Schedule. That is why you have an administrative schedule to leverage. For example, you wouldn't list, "Interview five web providers, shortlist to three, and then evaluate based on references and price before hiring one." Those details belong in your administrative schedule.

For Philip and Edwin, we tackled things at a bird's-eye view. One milestone was securing land, but we didn't list anything further, even though dozens of steps would go into making that milestone possible.

That keeps the business plan uncluttered and easy to evaluate, both for you and for any reviewers.

Finally, be sure you start your Schedule timeline in the past. Include a quick view backward that shows the biggest milestones you have already completed. One way to do this is by including a simple line that indicates the current and previous months. That can span back from weeks ago to years ago and should snapshot important milestones you already hit. This is important in order to show momentum.

Technical Layout

Your Schedule should be clean and simple. It should be skimmable and show simply what has been done and what milestones are on the horizon. It should also be segmented by months, quarters, or years. Segmenting by quarters is often the right view, although as I'll show you in a moment, sometimes the annual view can make sense like it did for AmaZone.

Schedule		Pajama Business LLC
Phase 1:	✓	Concept clarity
Completed	✓	Logo / brand prototyping
(Q1 Year)	✓	Consumer landscaping
	✓	Entity establishment
	✓	Initiate business launch plans
Phase 2		Entity adjustment (LLC-Partner)
(Q2 Year)		Landlord – solidify lease term
		Refine architecture planning
		Budget refinements
		Investor / capital secure
Phase 3		Permits and licenses
(Q2-3 Year)		Existing customer notice
		Project initiation: materials orde
		Project management: structure
		Project finalization: aesthetics
		Marketing for relaunch
Phase 4		Relaunch: Grand Open
(Q3-4 Year)		Budget adjust - actual CapEx
		Budget adjust - actual OpEx
		Operational rhythms / refine
Phase 5		Concept clarity
(Year+)		Expansion planning
		Feasibility study: new location

It doesn't matter in which order you complete your administrative schedule versus your big-picture schedule. You can build your administrative schedule first and then use it to group bigger line items for the Schedule section of your business plan. Or you might find it easier to work backward, building the big milestones first and then reversing to an outline of the smaller administrative items you would need to complete to accomplish those milestones. Whichever way feels most comfortable for you is fine.

To get you started with the administrative and big-picture schedules, consider these prompts to help you brainstorm your milestones.

Several months ago, our business was at this stage:
(Suggestions: product development, purchased marketing materials)

1.

2.

3.

Today we have completed:
(Suggestions: gathered licenses/permits, met with a lawyer to file for incorporation)

1.

2.

3.

In the upcoming months/year, we expect to accomplish:
(Suggestions: find an office space, hire personnel)

1.

2.

3.

Finishing the AmaZone Schedule

When I worked on the schedule for AmaZone, I had a huge challenge showing the business in the best light. The team had a long way to go before launching the business. However, they had already come well past the halfway point in many areas. Offering a glimpse at all they had done while still being transparent about the milestones ahead meant I needed to create a more visual—yet extremely simple—schedule for the business plan.

AMAZONE
THEME PARK
NEW YORK

Timeline

The business concept has been in development for more than a decade. The fruits of these efforts have led to this point of final planning and implementation. The next five years will yield important milestones, including land secure, fund-raising, and construction of the vision.

Final concepting is underway now with architecture and feasibility study in critical phases today. The timeline for Grand Open in 2021 is contingent on land secure no later than December of 2018. If secured sooner, the timeline will benefit accordingly.

Once land is in possession of AmaZone, early sales of luxury townhouses will benefit the project and will start revenues for the business. Note: The financials show a conservative scenario where townhome sales are not started until the AmaZone is ready for Grand Open.

Grand Open will occur in Spring 2021.

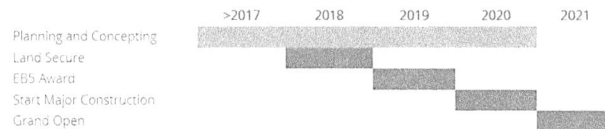

A Truly "Grand" Opening

At the grand opening, indigenous people from the Amazon will be flown to New York to perform and play music. The culture of the Amazon will flood the New York block and create an immersive experience for anyone visiting the AmaZone theme park.

Schedule

	>2017	2018	2019	2020	2021
Planning and Concepting					
Land Secure					
EB5 Award					
Start Major Construction					
Grand Open					

Instead of separating the multiple points where planning and conceptualizing would need to occur, I simply made it an ongoing task in the Schedule. The plans have changed and would continue to change over time. I didn't want to negatively impact the schedule with the reality that "if this happens, then we can do that" or "depending on how the outcome of this one thing goes, we can then move in this direction."

Instead, I focused on the absolute knowns. For instance, "Land Secure" was an inevitable milestone. Even if the desired plot of land near Coney Island was not granted to the AmaZone team, they would pivot and find a new location. In general "Land Secure" was an absolute step in this process, even though there was uncertainty about where that land would be.

Hyper-simplifying this Schedule section is extremely important and can be harder to do for more complex businesses. Had AmaZone had a more detailed schedule up front in the business plan, investors would easily be overwhelmed by all the what-ifs that would be implied. Overwhelming readers at the business plan stage can leave a bad taste in their mouths at the start, hurting AmaZone's odds for funding.

The business plan wasn't meant to sell investors on offering $500 million right away. It was simply meant to educate, inform, and hopefully entice investors to seek more information and interaction with Philip and Edwin about further details. After looking at the business plan, the investors can have additional conversations that may include looking at the administrative schedule and understanding the core pivot points and variables with this business launch. However, introducing those elements too early, in the business plan phase, may deter investors because of all the overwhelming uncertainty of what could happen in the future.

Showing the timeline in this way led to a clean representation of the intentions for AmaZone. It was simple enough to understand. Everyone, from investors to city officials to possible partners, was able to gather the overall direction for launch, even though it spanned five years.

Don't Get Stuck: How to Get Started

Your Schedule can start with what you have already done. Think back to the activities you've already completed for your business. Use them as a starting point and then think through the current action items you are working through. With this momentum, keep thinking forward to the next step and the next. Note that your Schedule view may be as short as 18 months or as long as three to five years. If you run out of known actions in that time window, then it's okay to stop at that point.

My Schedule Section includes:

- ❑ My Administrative view
- ❑ My Big-Picture view

You're Ready for the Home Stretch!

You are in the final chapters of this book and the final stages of finishing your business plan! Congratulations! Over the next three chapters, I'm going to move from client stories to expert advice. You will get help and guidance not just from me but from three experts in risk analysis, financial strategy, and investor perspective. The three gurus who contributed to the next chapters are held in high regard in their fields, and I'm so excited to be able to give you direct access to their personal, unbiased advice so you can finish your business plan strong.

In the next chapter, you will conduct a simple SWOT Analysis. SWOT is strengths, weaknesses, opportunities, and threats that apply to your business. While it is a straightforward exercise, most businesses overlook their true risks and threats and make mistakes on how they approach their strengths and opportunities. The following chapter will help you stay on the right path for each component of your SWOT Analysis.

Chapter 9

Outlining the Strengths, Weaknesses, Opportunities, and Threats in Your Business

Every business owner needs to know three essential components: you need to understand the market, understand the strategy, and understand the financials. Without these things, or with the lack of clarity on any one of these, then you are going to have problems.

—Ishmel Sanchez, founder and CEO, CapStratum Management LLC

I n this chapter, you will get invaluable advice from someone who has a personal barometer for what makes a person successful. Ishmel Sanchez has unique insights and tends to leave you in awe in a few different ways. Beyond being humble and unassuming, Ishmel has earned pure respect from many in the world of entrepreneurship with his clear success as a business tycoon. With straightforward common sense and a sixth sense for business, he's one of those people who brings infinite value.

His company, CapStratum Management LLC, is a financing and investment firm that focuses on lower to mid-market companies with annual revenues of $10 million and earnings before interest, tax, depreciation, and amoritization (EBITDA) of $3 million or higher. His business helps companies who are seeking anywhere from $5 million to hundreds of millions in investment. He helps entrepreneurs who are looking to grow their businesses strategically, sometimes by acquiring other businesses in the industry. His company invests, syndicates for joint investments, and coordinates needs with hedge fund providers and other investing businesses. Simply put, he helps great businesses reach their full potential with the capital and strategic investment partner they need.

Since he deals with larger amounts of risk, his ability to understand the strengths, weaknesses, opportunities, and threats of a business is paramount. Making sure a business has a clear growth path and that the business owner is capable is critical for each of Ishmel's projects. While he handles more existing businesses than start-ups, he still prides himself on having a clear gauge for what makes a successful business, no matter what stage of growth it may be in at the moment.

I collaborate with Ishmel from time to time to build out business plans for some of his select clients. When he first reached out to me, it was obvious that his clients were of a really unique caliber. I asked him a bit about how his process works and how he finds such promising businesses to invest in. Aside from prescreening his entrepreneurs with a simple questionnaire, he has also gained a good understanding of what an entrepreneur with potential looks like. With their personality, attitude, and attention to detail, he has gotten really good at being able to tell a promising business venture from a bad deal, often just from a one-on-one encounter with the business owner.

The biggest struggle entrepreneurs have with a risk assessment is lack of clarity on what would cause them to fail. Conducting a strengths, weaknesses, opportunities, and threats (SWOT) analysis requires them to gain clarity on their gaps and advantages. Ishmel's clients are driven, motivated, and inspired. When I asked him if those were the qualities that defined someone's advantages for success, he agreed that they were important qualities but said they weren't the core drivers of a business's success. He said start-ups in particular need the following advice:

- Know your own capabilities and limitations.
- Know that you need the right people at the right time to be on your team (doing the right tasks for their skill sets).
- Keep your business uncomplicated; meet a need, and meet it simply.
- Don't let doubt hold you back; use it as an area where you need more knowledge.
- Keep your purpose and drive in focus; it will motivate you through the difficult moments.

Each of these components plays a role in your risk and chance for success. There is a way to leverage each one in your SWOT Analysis. Approaching your SWOT risk assessment with awareness and an open mind will help you reveal the clear areas your business needs to consider.

Let Me Be Honest with You

The SWOT Analysis section is very deeply misunderstood by both inexperienced and experienced entrepreneurs. However, this misunderstanding is not always completely the entrepreneur's fault. I've seen descriptions and instructions for SWOT Analyses that are thoroughly confusing and even contradictory. In this chapter, we will unpack a SWOT Analysis simply and clearly to avoid confusion.

Finishing a SWOT Analysis requires the business owner to think from slightly unnatural perspectives, which can feel so uncomfortable that it distracts from the exercise. However, it is a very simple part of your business plan that can bring impactful benefit to your overall strategy. For this reason, I will try to help you understand the right angle to approach each section from, with the goal of making it less awkward and less uncomfortable. With Ishmel's advice in mind, let's consider how to create a powerful risk assessment of your business by conducting a great SWOT Analysis.

The Goal of Your SWOT Analysis

The goal of your SWOT Analysis is to understand your business factors internally and externally. It is meant to show how you may be affected by what happens inside and outside your business. While it's not as detailed as the STEEPLE Analysis you already conducted in your Micro Research section, it is just as important to the overall health of your strategy.

Impact of This Section for Investors

Investors will review your SWOT Analysis for depth and self-awareness. They will look at the information to gauge your understanding of the market factors that may influence you, and they will look at how you view your organization's internal pros and cons. Here's what they want to know: Is this entrepreneur looking at the business environment with rose-colored glasses? Or do they clearly realize the areas where their business has the most power and vulnerabilities?

Impact of This Section for Bankers

Bankers will review your SWOT Analysis for knowledge of where your business has weaknesses and how you plan to address them. They will be interested to know what your mitigation plan is for the threats to your business in the near future. For bankers, the question will be whether your overall risk is high or low based on your internal and external factors.

Impact of This Section for Strategy

Your business strategy will be directly influenced by this SWOT Analysis. Ironically, it is hard to conduct a thorough SWOT Analysis until you have a basic business strategy to analyze. Now that you have completed your market research and internal operations plan, you are well positioned to bounce it against a simple SWOT Analysis to see where any lingering strategy gaps may exist. After completing this section, you may find you want to go back to your Operations section to make some tweaks to your plans based on what you find here.

Creating a SWOT Analysis

Your SWOT Analysis will consist of four sections to address. Each section will be specific to either internal perspective or external perspective.

- Strengths – Internal
- Weaknesses – Internal
- Opportunities – External
- Threats – External

The Strengths and Weaknesses pertain to factors that hurt or help your business from the inside. The Opportunities and Threats focus on factors that happen to you because of factors outside of your business. Let's review each of these four factors.

Understanding Your Strengths

Strengths in a SWOT Analysis ask you to list the advantages that are unique to your business. These are things like the following:

- Having a team member or partner who has launched a successful business.
- Having a proprietary element to your business that is legally protected (e.g., a patent).
- Having a free service or offering (e.g., website build, office space, vehicle, etc.) to use thanks to a unique circumstance.
- Having unique information that will benefit your business (e.g., survey results, research and development outcomes, technology platform, other information you solely have that no one else has generated or has access to).
- Having something that only your company has as an asset (e.g., personnel, equipment, location, etc.) that gives you a special competitive advantage.

Some entrepreneurs stay too generic with this step. They may include "we have a good CFO." However, your competitor may also have a good CFO, so what would make yours shine brighter? What specific accomplishments has your CFO made? What notoriety has he or she received, or what experience has he or she gleaned that will directly impact your business positively? List those traits and accomplishments specifically.

When Ishmel spoke about offering a business solution in an uncomplicated way, this aligned perfectly with where start-ups shortchange their own offerings. You may find that one of your internal strengths is that you have figured out how to provide a service or product that is highly simplistic, very easy to market, or insanely inexpensive to produce. These elements are definitely strengths, and the more simplistic they are, the more likely that they are a core strength for your business.

Once you list each of the Strengths for your company, add another sentence or two explaining how you plan to maximize those strengths to benefit your business. Did your CFO launch a similar business in the past? Great! Perhaps you can maximize that by not just having this superstar overlooking your financials but perhaps by also working with that CFO to outline a strategy plan based on what he or she knows. Purposefully talking through someone's perspective, recommendations, and opinions can be more impactful than simply sticking that person in a role and hoping he or she brings success to your business. It's also a great way to demonstrate your appreciation and respect for that person as a team member, which is a great way for any start-up to build positive morale.

Or perhaps you don't have a stellar CFO on your team. In fact, maybe you know you desperately need one. If that's the case, you will want to list that in your Weaknesses section.

Revealing Your Weaknesses

Your business weaknesses are likely many if you are a start-up. However, that's not a bad thing, and you do not need to list all of them here. You will simply list the things internally that are unique gaps to your business. These things may include the following:

- No CFO or person on the team who is comfortable with financials.
- Not having a necessary feature in your product or service that your competitors have.

- Being in a less-than-ideal location compared to your competitors.
- Having a gap in capital that you don't have the line of sight to close.
- Having a negative internal relationship where there is frequent, unhealthy conflict.

Remember that these weaknesses are meant to be unique to your business. This is not a place to list the common weaknesses that apply to every business or start-up. For instance, you wouldn't mention "no logo," "no branding," or "no sales yet" if you are a start-up. Those are not weaknesses; they are simply milestones that any new business needs to tackle.

You may find that this section challenges you to admit the weaknesses you as a business owner bring to the business. One of Ishmel's pieces of advice is to clearly know your own weaknesses. That may mean that you are not the best person to be in charge of marketing, hiring and firing personnel, or performing other key tasks in the business. Be sure to be honest with yourself about your own limitations. That way, you can hire the right people to fill those gaps.

Once you have a list of weaknesses, you should add a sentence after each one that would eliminate that weakness and the ways you would accomplish that. With the CFO example, the obvious way to fix this weakness is to bring an experienced person to the team or send a current team member for training. However, some weaknesses will be more challenging to handle. Consider brainstorming with someone you trust if you feel you are stuck on where solutions may be hiding.

If you find you have multiple ways to fix a weakness and can't decide which one would be best, add those to your Operations plan or Schedule as a specific goal with a deadline. That way, you will be able to move on, but keep that weakness at the forefront of your business to-do list. The goal is to mitigate or minimize as many internal weaknesses as you can.

Once you have your internal weaknesses listed and a plan on how to eliminate or address each one, you can move on to the great opportunities that will benefit your business.

Maximizing Your Opportunities

Now that you are done with your internal factors, it's time to shift gears and think about external factors. Some people find this hard to do, although they already have a solid starting point. Revisit your STEEPLE Analysis because you may want to pull an opportunity from there to use here.

Opportunities that are external and affect your business will be listed in this section. You will have a chance to review your environment for what may positively impact your business. These factors can be large or small and can apply to just your business or to your overall industry. Here are some examples:

- Local permitting office is removing the restriction on signage next year, so we can place a large, bright LED sign, which will help increase traffic to and awareness of our store.
- A competitor just announced that they are going out of business, so we can easily capture some of their customer base.
- A blog post was released in *Forbes* that drives organic traffic to our products.
- A new industry conference is launching, so we will buy a ticket to attend and connect with vendors and potential customers.
- Our manufacturing provider is shifting to an energy-efficient facility, so we will be able to claim that we use an LEED-certified green manufacturer.

One word of caution: try to seek opportunities that are as specific to your business as possible. There should be one or two points that help your business, not your competitors or the broader industry. You also want each opportunity to have an action item or outcome associated with it.

As you work through your external opportunities, also consider how they align or support the overall mission and vision of your company. Ishmel recommends that you keep those personal and business goals at the forefront of your mind to help you stay focused. When thinking through your business opportunities, also think through how the goals you have are directly affected positively by external opportunities. Add those goal-supporting external opportunities to your SWOT Analysis.

For the next and final part of your SWOT Analysis, you will work through the external factors that pose threats to your business.

Mitigating Your Threats

Once again, you may have already done some of this work in your STEEPLE Analysis. Now you will think through the external threats that can impact your business negatively. You will consider what things are truly beyond your direct control, and you will try to look for ways to mitigate the risks of those factors. Here are a few examples:

- There is a new data privacy law that will impact our current customer information system next year, so we will update our e-mail lists now and start working to transition to a new data-compliant provider.
- A new high rise being built across the street will obstruct our storefront access to street traffic, so we will work on getting permission to construct a new street-front sign to help people see us better from the main road.
- A new competitor from another country has copied our main product and is selling it at a far lower price, impacting us and our competitors. So we will launch a new awareness campaign showing the quality differences and recommitting to our relevance factors, which will increase customer loyalty and retention.
- A new sales tax rate will go into effect next quarter, so we need to find one percent in cost reductions in order to avoid raising our prices before the new tax rate goes live.
- The cost of steel is being impacted by a new tariff, so we will work to find an alternative to steel that will be more cost-effective.

Just like your Weaknesses factors, you want to list a mitigation plan for each of these threats that are present for your business. Simply identifying the problem is only half the equation. There may be some items in your Threats section that you cannot answer or address right now; add them to your Schedule or Operations section as to-do items to mitigate or tackle soon.

One of the qualities Ishmel mentioned was that a success-destined entrepreneur never accepts ignorance or self-doubt as a reason for inaction. Remember, if you are unsure of what to do next or how to mitigate a problem, you should view it as an area where you need to learn. You may not know how to mitigate an internal weakness or external threat, or you may have serious doubts about making the right decision, but that simply means your action is to figure out what *is* possible. Research and dig for answers to what you are unsure about, and you will find yourself in a great position if you adopt that mindset.

With this final element in your SWOT Analysis, you now have the finished components to your risk management plan. There is risk in not making the most of the positives and risk in not being aware of how to handle the negatives. With your clarified strengths, weaknesses, opportunities, and threats—with clear actions tied to each factor—you have effectively designed a simple risk evaluation for your business.

Things to Avoid

Your SWOT Analysis can only be helpful if you create actions around each factor. If you are unsure about whether your maximization plans for your Strengths and Opportunities are strong enough or whether your mitigation plans for your Weaknesses and Threats are specific enough, take a moment to frame them as SMART goals. Make sure every factor has a maximization or mitigation plan that is specific, measureable, attainable, relative, and time-bound. That way, you will be able to add clear actions to each element in your SWOT Analysis, which will become the risk management plan for your business.

Technical Layout

The technical layout for your SWOT Analysis can be shown a couple of different ways. You may have seen a four-square model where you list the strengths in one square, weaknesses in another, and so on. That is

SWOT Analysis

Pajama Business LLC

Strengths

One of our founding members launched Snuggie, and we will work with him to create a target customer profile so we can market specifically to that niche with his advanced understanding of the apparel market.

SMART GOAL:

Quarterly strategy sessions with CMO for marketing actions and tracking effectiveness for customer persona

Weaknesses

Our core web developer left the team, so we no longer have an in-house resource for web development. This will be an added cost. We are going to list an ad for hiring a new part-time developer so we can maintain progress, which is all we can afford at this time. We will transition to one or two full-time developers by quarter 2 when sales reach $100K.

SMART GOAL:

Hire an experienced developer at a part time salary of $40K a year by June 5th to stay on schedule

Opportunities

A new study found that more work-from-home professionals will be expected to conduct remote meetings inclusive of video, which will help market demand for our product. This timing means we need to enter the market by the first of the year to capitalize on first-to-market advantage at the beginning of the time when this trend is taking hold.

SMART GOAL:

Product and marketing launch in December to gain traction during the holidays and start the new year with initial brand reputation in place by Q1

Threats

The fiber material we use to create the soft quality in our pajamas is no longer going to be supported by our supplier due to limited availability. We need to find an alternative or will need to find an unlimited supply of the material with a new vendor.

SMART GOAL:

Launch a new R&D effort to test new fabric options to replace the soft texture of our current product line. Develop an R&D budget by next quarter and initiate the plan and schedule for managing that new department.

okay for brainstorming, but it does not lend much room for formulating goals and actions. If you are planning to use your SWOT Analysis for a banker or investor, I recommend that you do this in short paragraph form. List one to three of your biggest factors in each category and really dig into how those factors will impact your business and how you will address each one. There will be more than one to three total factors, but you will whittle them down to the most pressing or most important factors to display in your business plan.

However, if you are working on your business plan for strategy, then you should consider listing the items in full and take the time to expound on each one wholly in your business plan. Brevity will not help you, and creating a comprehensive SWOT Analysis and keeping it in its complete form in your business plan will be powerful. It may run two to three pages depending on the number of factors you have identified.

Don't Get Stuck: How to Get Started

If you feel stuck in starting your SWOT Analysis, go back to your Schedule section. Take a look at each milestone and ask yourself whether there are any internal strengths your business has that will help with this goal. Think about whether any internal weaknesses may hold you back or impact whether you can meet that timeline. Brainstorm what types of external factors may help or hurt your chances of meeting that schedule line item the way you intend. Use this method for each item in your Schedule to get the ball rolling on your SWOT Analysis.

Now that your risk assessment is behind you, it's time to map out the numbers to your vision. The next chapter will walk you through creating financial forecasts that make sense for your business. You will be able to use the handy financials template that accompanies this book, and you will create forecasts for your business that will reveal what it will take to be a profitable company.

My SWOT Analysis includes:

- ❑ My internal strengths
- ❑ My internal weaknesses
- ❑ My external opportunities
- ❑ My external threats

Chapter 10

Financials

When you take your profit first, it's similar to the concept of paying yourself first, but it's <u>not</u> a budgeting tool – it's an accounting hack. Behaviorally, it changes everything. It forces you to do more with less.

—Corbin Cook, founder SMB Strategy Consultants

www.smbstrategyconsultants.com

W hen I first found out what Corbin Cook does for business owners, I was floored. I had no idea a service like his even existed. His company, SMB Strategy Consultants, helps businesses with profit strategy in various ways. Sometimes, his company guides business owners during challenging times in growth cycles, and sometimes it supports the preparation for eventual buyout as part of an exit strategy. The service I was most struck with is akin to a fill-in CFO role in which he works alongside business owners to make them more profitable. Most business owners need this at one time or another— just another set of experienced eyes on things, uncovering issues and offering fresh perspective.

Corbin is one of those people who radiate passion, and I felt it from our first phone call. I initially was in touch with him to see how we could collaborate professionally. I was also seeking services that I could refer to my clients. I get a healthy mix of businesses that are in the start-up phase and existing businesses that are growing. SMB Strategy Consultants fills a void by offering a hands-on, personalized solution for business owners who need clear guidance.

Seeing Corbin's methodologies showed me that I had been thinking about business plan financials completely wrong. When we first began communicating, I felt like I understood financials pretty well. After all, I've done my share of business plans, budgets, and forecasting. I understand the relationships between balance sheets, income statements, and cash flows. I've done estimating and forecasting in the corporate world. In fact, those were among my core duties when I left my position with GE to focus on Written Success full time. I definitely would say I know numbers.

So when Corbin showed me I was focusing on profit the wrong way, it felt like a huge revelation. He explained that his tactics include working with clients to put profit first and then working backward. Instead of the traditional equation that says "cost + profit = price," he said simply, "Flip it. Determine your margin, then set your price, and what's left is the cost you need to get to." It really is simply brilliant.

Plus, he added more color to the idea of owner salaries. I shared with him how hard it is sometimes to get entrepreneurs of start-ups to agree to take a salary. They believe that every dime should go back into the business and that they should only get paid if the business gets paid. So when they build their business plan financials and when year one shows a loss, the owner is quick to remove his or her salary as the first place to cut costs.

This is a huge mistake that Corbin has to correct with his clients. He shared that he makes it a priority to evaluate the owner's salary first and foremost when starting with a new client. He makes sure they are not just taking a salary but that they are taking home a paycheck that's fair and appropriate for what an owner should be paid, as well as quarterly dividends.

I felt like his approaches to business financials were game-changing. I remember taking a fresh look at a business plan I was working on and deciding to create a second set of forecasts. The duplicate forecasts were built by starting with desired profit first and then working backward, giving the owner a fair salary. Sure enough, the financials came out differently. When I was forced to back into costs, it also forced me to think more creatively about where to lower costs in order to meet the goal. I ended up with bigger profits and lower costs, while still using very competitive prices.

Can you remember a time when you worked through building something but didn't have the right tool or information to do it perfectly? Maybe it was hanging a picture with a thumbtack instead of a picture hook, or using a towel to open a jar instead of a rubber pad or proper jar opener. For me, learning these insights from Corbin was like finding the perfect tool for my project. Armed with his insights, I was able to develop more solid, profit-laden projections for my clients. With these new concepts, every business plan I worked with after that was notably different. The new approach impacted the balance sheet, income statement, and cash flows. It impacted the investor returns and the overall health of the business.

Creating financials can be the hardest part of creating a business plan. Usually, you don't have any idea what revenues you may have when you're a new business owner. You also feel lost when thinking about what your costs may be or what your profits may look like. Part of my job is to help work through that, and now I'm able to do it more strategically than ever.

Let Me Be Honest with You

Creating financial projections is a mix of art and science, and you will never get them right. Forecasts are always wrong. You cannot get around this. There is no correct revenue number to get to. You cannot fortune-tell the future of your business with complete accuracy, which is okay. Your goal is to simply paint the picture of what you are working toward. If you create projections that are too weak or too aggressive, then you risk setting yourself up for failure. That is why your financials should be finished very strategically.

The biggest struggle entrepreneurs have with the financials is figuring out where to start. In this chapter, I'll go through some terms and concepts so you can understand the basics of developing financial projections. I also encourage you to leverage the template that accompanies this book, which will auto-populate your financial projections with graphs and charts that you can use in the main sections of your business plan.

The Goal of Your Financial Forecasts

Business plan financials are an estimate of your business's health in the future. You are simply making a logical prediction of your business potential. Your business plan financials need to include, at minimum, a cash flow statement, balance sheet, and income statement. These financial statements should span three years from start-up. Many templates and guides are over-built and created to mirror financials for an existing business, not a start-up. I'll show you what you really need to include and will share the small nuances you need to include if you are using your business plan for funding.

When I first started building financials, it took quite a few before I realized how everything fits together. When you create financials correctly, the numbers should "walk." The financial statements should correlate in specific ways and tell the story of the business with numbers. And, of course, using Corbin's methods has helped get to the strongest story possible for every business I support. I'll share some insights about that process now.

Impact of This Section for Investors

Your financials are usually the most important section for investors. When you are building a business plan for investors, you need to show where your clear break-even point is, the year and month you will become profitable, and when they might see a return on their investment. They may be evaluating your plan for a high-growth potential, so strong growth year-over-year may be what they look for the most.

You should know that all investors have their own perspective of what is most important in a business plan forecast. There is no hard, fast rule that one financial statement is more important or more telling than another, although some investors will swear that all the answers are in cash flow or that you can only tell the true health of a business based on the balance sheet. So when you share your financials with an investor, expect him or her to ask questions, and then view it as a good thing. They will only ask questions about a business that they are genuinely interested in.

Impact of This Section for Bankers

Your business plan financials will be reviewed by underwriters when you submit your plan for a bank loan. The underwriters will want to see steady and stable growth that shows you have a realistic and modest way of developing the business. They want to see predictable scenarios based on attainable goals. Try to avoid projections that show explosive growth or highly aggressive sales targets. They will want stable profits that show you will have the ability to repay the loan comfortably, and they will want to see that you are working on a low-risk, low-volatility growth plan.

For a bank loan submission, the template that accompanies this book also has a loan amortization schedule you can include with your business plan. Simply plug in the desired loan term and interest rate, and it will automatically update in your financials.

Impact of This Section for Strategy

Many entrepreneurs work their financials napkin-style. Maybe all you have done so far is something on a whiteboard, in a notebook, or a scenario in an Excel sheet. Maybe the calculations are just in your head, or maybe you haven't really envisioned the financial side of your business yet. That's okay, wherever you are. This is a time when you need to keep yourself honest. You will answer questions such as these: Is this really going to be profitable? Am I able to live on the budgeted owner's salary? Do I have enough money to cover start-up costs?

This is also a place where strategy shifts are likely to occur. When you put everything on paper and can see whether your current idea makes enough money in theory, you can make adjustments to how you will execute in more profitable ways. You can challenge yourself on whether you thought of everything or missed a few points in your vision. You will fill in more blanks and work through the last of your business gaps by the end of your financials. For that reason, this is often the most clarifying section for entrepreneurs building their plan solely for strategy.

Creating Financial Forecasts

A client once told me, "I don't need financials in my business plan because the business doesn't exist yet." Financials are forecasts, projecting into the future. If you plan for your business to have a future, then plan to develop projections!

I'm going to show you the most simplistic way to develop business plan financials using the template provided with this book. You don't need an MBA or business education to do financials. Most people fall on one end of the spectrum, either feeling completely helpless with the idea of creating forecasts or comfy with numbers with a tendency to overcomplicate projections with way too much detail. Regardless of which end you are on, the real problem is that most templates are very manual or have questionable methodology that aligns more with accounting than forecasting. This only complicates things for most people, and they plug in inputs they don't understand.

It's more important to create financials that are easy to update during the next months than it is to get them close to accurate at the start. Most of your forecast variables will be uncovered as you actually start taking action, so it's natural that these costs and incomes morph a bit as you move forward.

Funds Needed: Your Asking Amount

The amount of funds you will need will be important to understand and list in your business plan. The included template gives you an option to use a calculation based on your inputs, so it will "walk" to a suggested funding amount for you. If you opt to use the number the template provides based on the costs you enter, then know that the number counts all of your costs and adds three months of your payroll and operational expenses. That creates the suggested funding amount.

However, if you are pursuing a bank or investor loan and want to list a different funding amount, you can simply enter the number you are seeking manually. Just know that the lender or investor will ask why you chose that number. If you stick with what the template provides as a suggested amount, then you can answer, "This asking amount covers my start-up costs plus three months of cushion as I get the business started."

If you are building financials for strategy, then consider the investment amount needed as an informational number. Use it to gauge your own ability to support this business in the event revenues begin later than expected. If you don't have the cash to support the business while it gets up and running, then consider options you have for getting funding or reducing your start-up costs.

Now let's walk through how to finish your financials with the template provided. The next section will start with the knowns, so you will fill in specific details you already know about your business. Then, we will cover how simply listing these knowns allows you to automatically have a completed cash flow statement, income statement, and balance sheet. Charts and graphs that will look great in your business plan are also included.

Known Numbers

The known numbers you already have are what you will start with. Things you've identified, such as how many people are on your team, whether or not you will need to buy land, and even utility bills, will be in your current knowledge base, thanks to all the research you've already done. Any small gaps such as average market salary for your

145

secretary and the cost to build a website can be addressed in a matter of minutes with simple Internet searches. Filling in every small gap will allow you to move on to your financial statements with ease and confidence in your assumptions.

This section will walk through simple steps to consider, following the format of the template that accompanies this book. Each step will represent a financial factor in your business, and each step is marked by a prebuilt table in the template. When you complete all steps, you'll be ready to look at modeling your forecasts based on those known numbers.

As you work through this section, you will want to make sure that you document any sources of information. You can do that on the Excel sheet by leaving a comment in the cell. For instance, if you research and find an administrative assistant makes an annual salary of $40,000 per year, you may enter that amount for your assistant salary and then add a comment to the cell that includes the URL of where you found that information. Or you can document it elsewhere, perhaps in an Appendix at the end of your business plan. You can call this Appendix "Financial Assumptions." It doesn't matter which method you use, as long as you are comfortable with it and document any data sources as you go. This will be important for your own reference later as you start buying things, hiring, and taking other actions in your business.

Financials will be handled in three parts. In "Part 1: Start-Up Costs," we will review the known numbers for your start-up costs. In "Part 2: Operational Costs," we will consider the known numbers for your monthly costs. Finally, in "Part 3: Revenue and Growth," we will tackle some simple estimates for your business revenues and growth.

Part 1: Start-Up Costs

Part 1 will include start-up costs for your business. It will require you to list any big items you plan to purchase and any land or buildings your business needs. It will also lead you to enter other start-up costs you expect to have for your business.

Step 1: List the Assets

The simplest way to think about assets is to view them as anything you might be able to sell later for cash. That could include equipment such as generators, vehicles such as work trucks, office equipment such as computers, printers, furniture, and more.

Note that land is considered an asset, too, but we are saving this for Step

Capital Expenditures / Start-Up Assets	Amount
Example Asset 1: Company Car	$20,000
Example Asset 2: Refridgerator	$1,000

3. So don't enter land here. I'll tell you why land is in a different step when we get to that section.

In the first table, you will list the assets you will need to start your business. Remember, assets are usually things that hold value and lose some of that value each year until they need to be replaced. An example is a car. If you buy a company car for $20,000, you may only plan to use that car for so many years before you need to replace it. In this table, list all known assets you will need in order to launch on day one of your business. If you are unsure about how much an item will cost, search online for an average and use that number as a reference.

Perhaps you also know you will need a refrigerator in your break room, and you expect you will need to pay about $1,000 for the model you want. Since a refrigerator is something you could likely get some cash for in a year or two if you decide to sell it, you can list it as an asset because it holds some value over time. Think about what assets your business will need to buy as it gets started. If you are seeking bank or investor funds, be sure to include any assets you plan to purchase with the borrowed money.

Step 2: Estimate Useful Years of the Assets

In the second table, list the number of years you can use each asset before you will need to replace it. This is a best guess, and you shouldn't feel that there is a wrong answer for these estimates. Once you have your years of use for each asset, you can then calculate how much you can claim in depreciation each year on your balance sheet.

Capital Expenditures / Start-Up Assets	Amount	Years of Use	Annual Depreciation
Example Asset 1: Company Car	$20,000	5	$4,000
Example Asset 2: Refridgerator	$1,000	10	$100

Using the car as an example, let's assume you plan to put 20,000 miles per year on the car for client visits and company-related travel. Perhaps you decide the car will only be in your possession for five years, and you plan to get a new car at year six when you hit 100,000 miles on the first car. You will enter "5" for years of use and divide $20,000 by five years. The answer is $4,000, or how much you can project for your depreciation amount each year. This number will impact your balance sheets, which will auto-populate in the template that comes with this book.

This is only an example for your own reference. Know that this template uses a straight-line depreciation method. There are multiple ways to depreciate assets for your business, but this is a simple approach that all banks and investors will easily understand. Other methods depend on guidelines that change from one tax season to another, and they are not necessary to consider at the business plan phase for most start-ups. Remember, your business plan is not an accounting statement; it is simply a guess at the future.

Step 3: List Land and Buildings

In this table, you will list any land or buildings your business will need to purchase in order to begin operating. Only list what will be bought and owned by the business. Do not list any leased space or rental property.

You may be wondering, "Isn't land an asset?" Yes, it is, but it is different than other assets. Here is why land is shown here instead of in your assets table in Step 1: It is an appreciating asset, not a depreciating asset. Over time, land typically gains value, not loses it, so you won't depreciate land on your balance sheet like you do for other assets.

Land	Amount
Example: Land (3 Acres)	$1,000,000

In this financials template, your land and buildings will be recorded as an asset on your balance sheet that neither gains nor loses value for the first three years. This is a conservative way to view the value of any property you need for the business. It assumes that its value will be stable in the short term and that you will be able to sell it for at least what you bought it for in a few years.

If you don't need to own land or a building to start your business, or if you plan to rent space, leave this blank. Any rental space costs will be shown in tables four and six.

Step 4: Other Start-Up Expenditures

You probably have a list of non-land, non-building costs that don't qualify as an asset. These costs belong in your Start-Up Expenditures table. This list

Capital Expenditures / Start-Up Non-Assets	Amount
Example 1: LLC establishment	$700
Example 2: Website developer	$1,000
Example 3: Patent application	$1,000
Example 4: Lease deposit	$5,000

includes things you will need to buy or pay for to get your business going. It can encompass costs associated with setting up your LLC, paying for a professional website, paying for a patent application, or putting first and last month's rent down on a space you want to lease.

Part 2: Operational Costs

In this part, we will work through costs that will occur monthly. This section includes payroll costs and requires you to add your

Monthly Payroll	Amount
Example 1: Owner Salary	$2,000
Example 2: Assistant	$1,500
Example 3: Marketing Admin	$1,750

own salary. It also covers monthly recurring bills you expect for your business.

Step 5: Monthly Payroll and Wages

Here is where you will list the team members you will need to pay (including yourself) and how much each person will be paid per month. During this next phase of your business, who will be on your team?

As you think about your employee costs, consider what the industry title is for each person. This will help you research salary ranges more accurately. For instance, when you think of hiring your assistant, think about what the industry calls that person. An administrative assistant? An executive assistant? An assistant manager? Each title will have a different salary, so consider each role carefully.

When you think about what your own salary should be, think about what you can reasonably live on considering your monthly expenses. Remember Corbin's advice that your salary should be fair for a business owner. For your first year, you may have a more modest salary, but year-over-year, your salary will grow with your profits. Simply make sure your first year's salary will cover your basic living expenses.

When you add monthly costs for payroll, do not get stuck trying to calculate taxes and unemployment allocation costs. These elements will become part of your budgeting later when you are operational. For now, keep it simple and focus on the big picture. These accounting-level details often derail entrepreneurs at this phase, and details tend to overcomplicate projections.

Step 6: Monthly Operational Expenses

Monthly Operational Expenditures	Amount
Example 1: Website maintenance	$250
Example 2: Cell Phones	$250
Example 3: Advertising	$1,500
Example 4: Electricity	$150
Example 5: Rent	$2,500

In this step, you will list the other ongoing costs your business will have each month. You will need to think through what other monthly costs your business will have. Think about the information you included in the Market Entry and Operational Strategy sections of your business plan. Then start listing the things that will become a business cost. What starting budget will you begin with to launch your marketing efforts? If you are renting a space, how much per month will you need to pay?

This section will prompt you to get serious and strategic about your answers. Any cost that is over-inflated will make it harder for you to be profitable. Any cost that is underestimated will risk unexpected cash problems later. This is where being very realistic will benefit you most. Where needed, do your research. If you don't know what the going rent prices are in an area you are considering, then search online for average cost per square foot for commercial rental property in the zip code you are considering. Take that number and multiply it by the square feet of space you will need. Or if you can find a property for rent that is similar to what you envision you will need, then use that rental listing as your baseline for your monthly lease payment. Whatever approach you take, be sure to list the source where you found that number in your Appendix or in a comment within the spreadsheet cell so you can find it again later.

Part 3: Revenue and Growth

This part guides you through entering your revenue expectations for the business. It also leads you to think about the growth potential for your business vision. At the end, you'll note that the last step shows you how to finalize your business plan financials.

Step 7: Monthly Revenue

This is the fun part. It's time to start thinking about income! You've already considered what your monthly payroll and monthly expenses will look like. Most entrepreneurs are on one end of the spectrum or the other. Either they have an idea in their mind of how much money their business will make, or they have no idea where to even begin estimating this.

If you already have a ball-park in mind, go ahead and plug that in to your monthly revenue line. If you have multiple streams of income,

Revenue	Monthly
Example 1: Pajamas	$5,000
Example 2: Mugs	$8,000

try to consider how much each revenue source might bring in for your business. For a smoothie business, that may mean having a separate revenue line for smoothies and a separate line for snacks. For a gas station, that might mean having groupings, where all food and drinks are one line item and gas sales are another line item. That should be relatively high-level and should be based on how many sales and at what price point you plan to make.

If you have no idea what your revenue may look like, try to estimate it, starting at a daily or weekly level. Your research may have uncovered industry averages you can consider. For example, industry averages show a car wash can expect one percent of traffic to stop for a car wash. For a street that has traffic counts of 20,000 cars per day, the business owner can expect an average of 200 cars to visit the wash per day. At $10 per car wash, that means the owner can guess that the car wash will have about $2,000 per day in revenue. If the wash is open seven days per week, that is $14,000 in revenue per week and $56,000 on average per month.

However, this ballpark has lots of nuances, doesn't it? For instance, people won't visit a car wash on rainy days. The number of hours per day the car wash is open will have an impact, too. What if the car wash is on a highway where people are going faster than 60 miles per hour and are unlikely to stop for a car wash? What if the car wash is in a location that is hard to see? All of these things become factors that will impact real revenue.

Because of all these factors, it can be easy to feel paralyzed—analysis paralysis, as it is often called. You need to stay diligent about your reality. Remember, you cannot predict the future; your projections will never be perfect. Your job right now is to get a baseline into your budget. Then work from that baseline. Considering the car wash scenario, perhaps the owner feels that $56,000 per month is not realistic for the vision of that business. To be more conservative, the owner might decide to take that baseline and reduce it by 20 percent. That is powerful because it is anchored to something. Simply picking a random number usually isn't helpful.

If the car wash owner is applying for an SBA loan and decides that $45,000 is a realistic revenue number for his projections, then there should be a baseline to consider. Underwriting will ask why his revenue makes sense. If he uses the industry average as a baseline and then reduces it by 20 percent to be conservative, he lands at $44,800. Now he can explain to the bank underwriters that he took a conservative approach in his projections by assuming that he should be able to earn at least 20 percent below what the industry average shows.

This applies to digital businesses in the same way. If you plan to launch an e-commerce business, for example, consider what your industry conversion is for marketing. If you are using targeted advertising, some industry standards say you can expect to convert at one percent for your ads and perhaps 10 percent for those who landed on your site or page. While those percentages vary widely by industry, product type, advertising medium, and ad effectiveness, the point is that there are industry averages. Pick the one most applicable to you and begin with that baseline. Then move it up or down based on factors and nuances you want to consider for your business.

Again, this will not be perfect or accurate. Try not to over-think this step. Get to a number and move on. You will likely adjust this later anyway, and until you list an estimated revenue, you cannot see how well it fits with the rest of your projections.

Step 8: Growth Plan

Your business will grow. Your costs and revenues will grow year-over-year as things move forward. This can be a diffi- cult thing to estimate, so the

Growth Plan	Year 2	Year 3
Revenue	15%	20%
Costs	8%	10%

template included with this book simplifies it quite a bit. To complete this, you need to think about how you hope to see your revenues grow in years two and three. If you plan to make $100,000 in year one, $200,000 in year two, and $300,000 in year three, then it translates to 100 percent growth in year two and 50 percent growth in year three.

There is also a place to list your cost changes. For some business- es, your costs will grow evenly year-over-year along with your rev- enues. So those businesses know that 50 percent revenue growth will equal 50 percent in cost growth, too. For most businesses, though, there are growth differences with costs and revenues. More revenues won't necessarily equal more costs. That is why you can change them independently.

If your business has other circumstances where cost of goods is more volatile month-to-month, or if you need support adjusting the assumptions to fit your exact situation, then consider outside help. Getting support to tailor the financial model so it fits your business perfectly is important. Having another set of eyes on your numbers is also good practice, even if you feel your numbers already make sense.

For professional business plan consultant support, start with www.writtensuccess.co for one-on-one help.

Optional Step 9: For Loan Requests Only – Loan Amortization Schedule

If you are sending your business plan to the bank or to an investor for a loan, you will also need to complete Step 9. You will plug in the number of years for the loan term you are seeking and interest rate you

Interest Rate	Loan Term (in Years)
5.00%	7

will need to repay the loan. For instance, with some types of loans and a decent credit rating, banks can offer loan terms of 10 years with 5 percent interest. Some investors like to see their money returned in less than five years with at least 7 percent interest. If you have clarity about your loan needs, you can enter the interest rate and loan term and paste this table into your business plan file. Otherwise, if this does not apply to you, just skip Step 9.

Step 10: Delete or Hide Red Rows

With all the previous steps completed, your projections are mostly complete. The inputs you added for each step are auto-fed to your cash flow, your income statement, and your balance sheet. Now it is time to click on the other tabs and delete or hide any red rows that are showing.

	Month 1	Month 2	Month 3	Month 4	Month 5	Month 6
Example 1: Pajamas	$ 5,000	$ 5,000	$ 5,000	$ 5,000	$ 5,000	$ 5,000
Example 2: Mugs	$ 8,000	$ 8,000	$ 8,000	$ 8,000	$ 8,000	$ 8,000
0	$ -	$ -	$ -	$ -	$ -	$ -
0	$ -	$ -	$ -	$ -	$ -	$ -
0	$ -	$ -	$ -	$ -	$ -	$ -
0	$ -	$ -	$ -	$ -	$ -	$ -
Total Revenue	$ 13,000	$ 13,000	$ 13,000	$ 13,000	$ 13,000	$ 13,000
Payroll Costs						
Example 1: Owner Salary	$ 2,000	$ 2,000	$ 2,000	$ 2,000	$ 2,000	2,000
Example 2: Assistant	$ 1,500	$ 1,500	$ 1,500	$ 1,500	$ 1,500	1,500
Example 3: Marketing Admin	$ 1,750	$ 1,750	$ 1,750	$ 1,750	$ 1,750	1,750
0	$ -	$ -	$ -	$ -	$ -	-
0	$ -	$ -	$ -	$ -	$ -	-
0	$ -	$ -	$ -	$ -	$ -	-
0	$ -	$ -	$ -	$ -	$ -	-
	$ -	$ -	$ -	$ -	$ -	-
TOTAL PAYROLL COSTS	$ 5,250	$ 5,250	$ 5,250	$ 5,250	$ 5,250	5,250
Monthly Operational Expenditures						
Example 1: Website maintenance	$ 250	$ 250	$ 250	$ 250	$ 250	250
Example 2: Cell Phones	$ 250	$ 250	$ 250	$ 250	$ 250	250
Example 3: Advertising	$ 1,500	$ 1,500	$ 1,500	$ 1,500	$ 1,500	1,500
Example 4: Electricity	$ 150	$ 150	$ 150	$ 150	$ 150	150
Example 5: Rent	$ 2,500	$ 2,500	$ 2,500	$ 2,500	$ 2,500	2,500
0	$ -	$ -	$ -	$ -	$ -	-
0	$ -	$ -	$ -	$ -	$ -	-
0	$ -	$ -	$ -	$ -	$ -	-
0	$ -	$ -	$ -	$ -	$ -	-
0	$ -	$ -	$ -	$ -	$ -	-
TOTAL OPERATIONAL COSTS	$ 4,650	$ 4,650	$ 4,650	$ 4,650	$ 4,650	4,650
LOAN REPAYMENT	$ 864	$ 864	$ 864	$ 864	$ 864	864
Total Cash Out	10,764	10,764	10,764	10,764	10,764	10,764
Shareholder Distributions for Income Tax (30%)	$ 671	$ 671	$ 671	$ 671	$ 671	671
Cashflow + / -	1,565	1,565	1,565	1,565	1,565	1,565
Period Beginning Cash Balance	$ -	$ 1,565	$ 3,130	$ 4,695	$ 6,260	7,825
Period Ending Cash Balance	$ 1,565	$ 3,130	$ 4,695	$ 6,260	$ 7,825	9,390

To allow room for as many entries as you need for costs and revenues, the template has extra rows. When you are finished with all of your assumptions, costs, and revenues and are ready to add the financials to your business plan, you will need to delete or hide all red rows throughout the template. That will allow you to paste the images of your financials into your business plan in a clean, neat way.

If you want to easily make changes later, I suggest you choose to hide rows rather than delete them.

To do this step, select a row by clicking the row number on the left side of the financials template. Then right-click and select either "Delete" or "Hide" to make that row disappear from view. The video that accompanies the financials template also walks you through this step with a live example, along with explaining how to paste each financial statement into your business plan.

Projections with Profit First

So far, you have built your projections based on siloed views of costs, revenues, and growth. Now that you can see how that translates to your cash flows, you can visualize whether your assumptions create a profitable business. Now is the time to ask what profit you want. Perhaps you won't be profitable in the first year, but by year two or three, what profits do you want to see for your business?

With that in mind, take another look at your revenues and costs. Are your revenues realistic, or could you expect higher revenues than what you listed by year three based on your growth plan? If they are completely realistic, consider creative ways you can reduce costs to widen your profit margin to your goal profit point by the third year. This is a good time to figure out how you can do more with less, as Corbin advises. Consider what revenues you need to increase or what costs you need to reduce in order to reach your goal.

After all, you are going into business to become profitable. If your financials do not reflect this, then your business plan will not be effective. As you work through any changes to cost, revenues, or growth, revisit the Operations and Market Entry sections of your business plan to make sure everything still aligns. Perhaps this exercise forces you to realize that you can price your products or services higher than you originally thought. Maybe you discovered that you can deploy a lower-cost marketing strategy in the first year or that you don't need to hire all personnel until year two. Also make sure adjustments like these are updated in the written section of your business plan.

Things to Avoid

If you feel like financials are not your strong suit or if you are uncomfortable with projections or don't feel familiar with Excel spreadsheets, that's okay. Try to avoid feeling intimidated by this and simply ask for help. This is one of those things where there are lots of ways to approach and complete the task. There are many schools of thought on financial projections, and for that reason, it can all be really overwhelming. Just know that having something is better than nothing and that an expert or professional can usually take a lot of the weight off of this process by guiding you down the best path for your specific business.

If you are pitching to a bank or investor, you should also avoid the expectation of instant approval or rejection. If you plan to show your financials to anyone—friends, family, partner, banker, investor—know that *they will challenge your numbers*. That is okay. It is not a bad thing. If anything, it simply means they are truly paying attention to your business plan.

Questions on your numbers, how you arrived at them, and so forth means your audience is trying to gain clarity, not trying to challenge or ridicule your approach. I've seen countless entrepreneurs become defensive when others ask questions such as these: "Why is year-two revenue so high?" "Why do you have a line item for this or that?" "Why don't you show payroll taxes?"

Instead, expect questions to come up. And when you respond, do so confidently. "Year-two revenues are so high because I project a 100 percent growth rate from year one to year two, and I have a line item for this or that because it is a needed cost or expense. I don't show payroll taxes because they are assumed in the overall cost of employee salaries for the sake of simplicity while forecasting." Sometimes, your answer will also be, "I picked that number as a placeholder until I have a better estimate available of the actual amount I need to list." It is okay to admit that something is simply your best guess for now.

Technical Layout

Now I will show you what the final financials will look like. The following is an example of a completed cash flow, income statement, and balance sheet. It will also review extra calculations that are included in your template.

Cash Flow

Below is a cash flow statement for one year. In your business plan, you will paste one year of cash flows on one page. Three years of cash flows will occupy three pages in your business plan. The cash flow shows month-to-month what your average income and expenses may resemble.

Income Statement

Your income statement is a condensed view of each year of activity. It will show the interest payments made on your bank loan (if applicable) and will show as a percent of sales how each expense impacts your financials. You can fit all three years on one page of your business plan.

	Year 1		Year 2		Year 3	
Cash Flows from Investing Activities	60,650					
INCOME	Amount	% of Sales	Amount	% of Sales	Amount	% of Sales
Gross Sales	156,000		179,400		215,280	
Net Income	$156,000		$179,400		$215,280	
EXPENSES						
TOTAL PAYROLL COSTS	63,000	40%	67,725	38%	74,498	35%
TOTAL OPERATIONAL COSTS	55,800	36%	59,985	33%	65,984	31%
* LOAN REPAYMENT	10,287	7%	2,484	1%	2,085	1%
Total Operating Expenses	129,087		130,194		142,566	
Net Profit (Loss)	$26,913		$49,206		$72,714	
*Loan payments omitting principal						

Balance Sheet

Your balance sheet will show overall company value at the end of each year. Your assets, outstanding loan amount, depreciation considerations, and other factors will display here. You should be able to fit all three years on one page of your business plan.

Other Calculations

The template has made other calculations for you. It calculates your overall margin and your accumulated cash flow, which are great additions you can consider for your business plan. These are found in the Graphs and Summary tab and come with visual charts. Consider adding these to your Financials section.

EBITDA (AND MARGIN)

ACCUMULATED NET CASH FLOW

	Year 1	Year 2	Year 3
Accumulated Cash In	$156,000	$335,400	$550,880
Accumulated Cash Out	$129,171	$259,386	$401,969
Net Accumulated Cash	$26,829	$76,014	$148,711

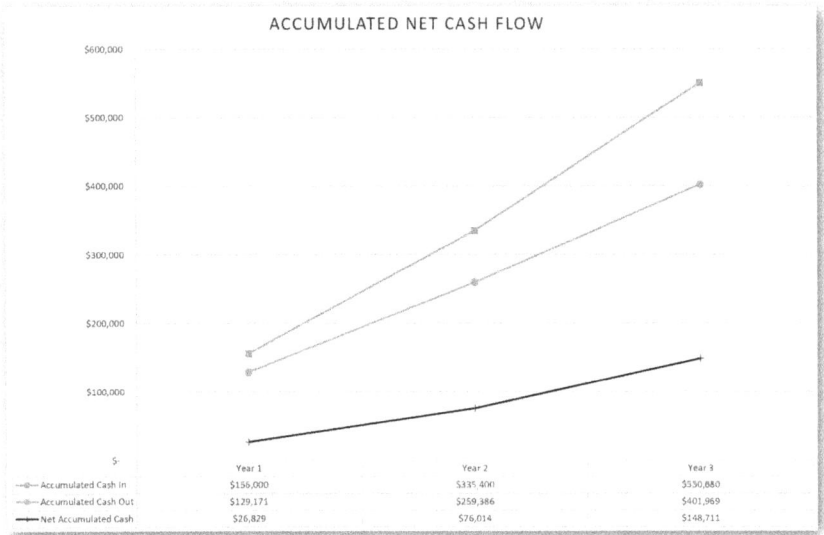

Don't Get Stuck: How to Get Started

To start your financials, your next step is to add your known numbers to the Financials template. Simply visit each table and plug in what you already have answers to. When you have listed everything you know, go back and fill in the blanks with research where needed.

Remember to add key assumptions and information such as where you found cost and salary information to your Appendix or in your financials Excel sheet. Documents and file items such as cost estimates from suppliers and web provider quotes or logo options or patent applications are things you may have collected to this point that would qualify as appendix items.

My Financials include:

- ❑ A list of assets
- ❑ An estimated number of useful years of the assets
- ❑ A list of needed land and buildings we will own
- ❑ A list of other start-up expenses
- ❑ A list of monthly payroll and wages costs

- ❑ A list of monthly operational expenses
- ❑ A list of monthly revenue streams
- ❑ An expenses and income growth plan
- ❑ Loan amortization schedule (for loan requests only)
- ❑ All red rows are hidden or deleted

Not the End

Alright, entrepreneur! You just worked through your entire business plan from beginning to end. You have completed a road map and strategy for launching your business, and because of your effort, you just increased your odds for success *big-time*!

However, this is not the end. This is the official beginning of your business, and this is where greatness starts. Your life will change, and your journey will shift as you launch your new business. And from one entrepreneur to another—I won't lie to you—it's going to be both exciting and terrifying at the same time, but the rewards are well worth the effort. Sincerest congratulations on your success thus far!

Now, if you are interested in pitching to investors, I have one more chapter for you. This bonus chapter will review some tips to consider if you plan to present your business idea for investor funding. Whether you already know your investor or you are simply open to using investor funds to start your business, the following will help you understand some basics so you can be more prepared for investor pitching.

Bonus Chapter

Preparing for Pitching to Anyone

Whether you intend to pitch your business plan for funding or partnership or simply for your own strategy, you should know that your finished business plan is extremely powerful. Many new entrepreneurs try to skip right to the pitch without having a full business plan first. However, if you plan to create a powerful pitch, it needs to be grounded in a finished business plan. Since you are here, at the end of this book, I assume you finished your business plan already.

This chapter will help you work through creating your pitch. Your pitch comes in two parts: a one-page elevator pitch and your presentation slides. The first is already done. Your elevator pitch is also known as a one-page business plan, and you created that in your Executive Summary. Now that your business plan is finished, you can pull that one- to two-page part out of your plan and present it separately as a first introduction to your business. Use this to get your investor excited before showing your full business plan or presentation.

The second part of your pitch is in slide format, which is what this bonus chapter focuses on. The presentation can be done in Microsoft PowerPoint, Apple's Keynote, or free online options. The following will review what investors want to see in your pitch, how to include the core components, and tips on the verbal content you need to be prepared for during your pitch.

What Investors Want to See

It never fails. If you pitch well, you'll be asked later to show your business plan. That means you need to have it all matching and harmonious so your audience will see consistency. Create your business plan first. That will be the hard part. When you are done, the content is there, so you simply have to take pieces of it and plop them strategically into a single-page document and presentation deck, and you will have an audience-ready pitch.

When you interview investors, they will have clear themes and expectations about what comprises a good investor pitch. One of the investors I trust is Aatif, a man who is incredibly intelligent and business-savvy by nature. Aside from a progressive blue chip corporate career, he is steeped in the world of investing and has some straight-forward advice for new entrepreneurs developing their pitch. His comments, which are similar to the thoughts of other investors I've worked with, are great guidelines to keep in mind while you are developing your investor pitch.

Investor Advice: Tip #1 – Know Your Market and Resources

When entrepreneurs are asked about the market they serve and the resources they need, a good response is specific and narrowed. Aatif notes that entrepreneurs lacking clear understanding of their market is an issue that comes up frequently. An entrepreneur will offer a broad industry need or vague resource needs, not realizing that the investor already has red flags about the response. Aatif offers the following sample scenario:

> Take starting an airline. Anyone can start one. I don't recommend it; it's one of the worst margin industries to get into, but anyone can get into the business. But your "resources" are planes, pilots, workers, and other people.
>
> And there are other details to consider with those resources. For instance, if they unionize, then they will eat into your margin.

And yes your "market" is other airlines, but your market is even buses. Because customers can choose to take a bus, can use another airline, or can drive on their own, these are also your competitors. They are the substitutions to your product and service. You need to know your market. If you don't do your research, your fail probability is high.

Aatif is more forgiving than some investors and may offer guidance and support during a pitch, telling you exactly what he wants to see and hear. However, many investors are less patient and don't have the same transparency. That means you may lose an investor with a broad industry description or vague list of business costs or start-up resources, but the investor may not directly communicate that this is the problem.

For your target market, try not to think of it in terms of who could buy your product or service. Instead, think of it in terms of which buyers would see your product or service as a perfect solution for their needs. Using the airline example, if your target audience is people taking a low-cost, no-frills transit option, then your market is no longer the entire airline industry. It's a specific subset of transportation providers targeting a specific buyer type.

After all, once you understand your true market, you can understand your growth potential in that space, which brings us to Tip #2.

Investor Advice: Tip #2   Know Your Scaling and Growth Plan
Your growth plan needs to be clear in your investor pitch. If your revenues go up in years two and three, then you need to be able to explain your plan for how that growth occurs for your business. You also need to understand whether that growth will pose additional challenges for your business. As Aatif notes, investors do not always see achieving huge growth as a smart approach.

> Sometimes an entrepreneur is in love with an idea, grows it too fast and scales it too quickly without using the right methodology to do it successfully, and they stretch themselves too thin.

To avoid the trap of presenting a bad scaling plan, make sure your pitch includes the following:

How you plan to grow and scale – Include marketing tactics, new revenue streams, and so on.

What that growth requires – Include costs, new personnel, additional space or buildings, and more.

The goal of that growth plan – To increase brand awareness for lower acquisition costs, to widen profit margins with low-cost revenue streams, to gain a competitive edge in a specific area over the competition, and so forth.

Investor Advice: Tip #3 – Present with Attention to Aesthetics

Your investor pitch should be easy to read and formatted with an intent to inform. Even with perfect content, your investor pitch can be viewed negatively if it is poorly formatted, too wordy, or feels haphazard. While investors like Aatif admit that a great presentation doesn't always equal a great investment deal, and vice versa, he still agrees that presentation is important.

> Having a strong presentation is important for raising any amount of money. It's one litmus test I use to see, "Can someone launch this business?" is "Can they actually do their diligence and research and put these concepts on paper?" If so, that's a good sign. But if you can't create a presentation and put in the effort at this step, then you won't be able to put in the work to the right level in the business later.

Your presentation should have consistency throughout for everything from font to terminology to color themes. With this book, you get a PowerPoint template that is preformatted for you. With this, you do not need to worry about the aesthetics; your focus will be on replacing it with the best content to describe your business.

That being said, you may be tempted to add long sentences, lots of images, or other components that can clutter the presentation. Consider these aesthetic tips to keep you focused:

- Less is more; aim for no more than five bullets in a text slide.
- Keep each bullet as short as possible, writing in note form, not full sentences.
- Try to avoid more than one photo image per slide to avoid visual clutter.
- Use charts and tables when possible when depicting financials.
- Keep your main presentation at 10–15 slides.
- Any additional content should be added as appendix slides at the end.

The layout of your pitch presentation will help the investor stay focused on the core components of your business and deal. Creating a simple presentation without too much information while including all the needed information is a very fine line to walk. However, when you keep simplicity in mind, you will find that you will have an investor-ready presentation finished in no time! Now, let's move on to what you must include in this simple presentation.

How to Include the Core Components

The core components of your presentation can be as few as 12 slides. After the first slide, which will be the cover of your presentation, and the second slide, which will be your table of contents, the rest will be the following 10 topics that you must include:

1. Summary Slide – Money needed, for what purpose, serving what industry.
2. Founders Slide – The founder and co-founder(s) of the business.
3. Market Slide – What market is serviced, location, the product mix in the market, etc.
4. Competitive Landscape – Your top three to five competitors and what their biggest strengths and weaknesses are.

5. Market Entry Strategy – How you plan to launch and facilitate the grand open.
6. Execution Plan – What you have already done in the business, and what steps are next.
7. Financials: Use of Funds – Show what you need investor funds for; a table format works well here.
8. Financials: Revenues – Great place to use your Revenue graph.
9. Financials: Expenses – Great place to use your Revenue graph.
10. Financials: Profit – Great place to use your Margin and earnings before interest, tax, depreciation, and amoritization graph.

Each slide should have the sole focus in the title of the slide. Be careful not to discuss costs when you are showing the revenue potential slide. Keeping each topic laser-focused will help your investor follow the presentation. I also recommend starting with a table of contents slide so your investor can see when points of interest occur in the presentation. Some investors will want to hyperfocus on market potential, others on costs, and others on the competitive landscape. Investors may be eager to jump to specific sections of interest, but showing where these key topics occur in your presentation up front can help them be patient as you run through each component of your pitch.

Now that you understand the flow of your presentation slides, let's touch on the topics that may come up during your verbal pitch.

Tips on Content

Your pitch is more than just your presentation slides. You may have noticed by now that you are leaving a lot of information out of your presentation. With narrowed topics, minimal text, and a short presentation, there is no way you can show the entire scope of your business in your slides alone.

That's okay. It's intentional. The slides are helpers for your verbal pitch. They are not meant to be the entirety of your pitch. For the content that investors will not see on your slides, you will need to speak about it, and you won't likely have a slide dedicated to the extra topics investors want to cover. This means you need to be ready with depth of knowledge for your own business.

Since you wrote your own business plan, you already know all the answers investors want to hear. You addressed them in your business plan, which your investor should get a copy of after your presentation pitch. This section will help you prepare for the most frequently covered verbal topics and questions that come up in pitches but that will be outside the scope of what you've written in your slide presentation.

Talking Point #1: Acquisition Strategy

Investors will likely ask about your acquisition strategy. They will want to know how you will get customers, convert customers, and generally let people know you exist. Investors are really curious about your ability to have a step-by-step plan for bringing your product or service to the people who need it the most.

If you have an offering that is truly new or unique, you will absolutely need to tell investors exactly how you plan to educate your potential customers. Be ready to explain your marketing plan in detail, including what platforms you will use, whether you will outsource help, and how many buyers your marketing is expected to produce.

Talking Point #2: What Regulations or Red Tape Will Apply

This is a huge test, and even the best intentioned entrepreneurs often fail it. When investors ask about regulations or red tape, they are asking you to explain the risks you already are aware of. They want your mitigation strategy where applicable. It pertains directly to your SWOT Analysis results. As a good appendix slide, you may consider adding your SWOT Analysis content if it makes you feel more prepared to talk about the risks and mitigation plan.

After you touch on specific risks and the mitigation plan you have for each one, you will need to show investors that you are still on the lookout for anything that would derail the business. Consider ending with a phrase such as this: "We are actively looking for other areas where risk may present so we can minimize it." Let them know that protecting your business is a priority, and that will tell them that protecting their investment is also a priority by default.

Talking Point #3: Growth Plan

The third frequently asked question is about your growth plan, just like Aatif referenced earlier in this chapter. Know that this is tricky territory, and your answer may not be what the investors have envisioned. Remember that this is somewhat subjective, and you want to defer respectfully to fully hear the advice and perspective of the investors to whom you are pitching. They may or may not have the best strategy, but you need to make sure you listen to their perspectives and thank them for offering their advice, whether you agree with the approach or not.

Some investors are adamantly for or against certain growth strategies, which can be an unexpected barrier during a pitch if they don't agree with your growth plan. You want your investors to see you as a partner who is open to new ideas and will be flexible when needed. One way to end your growth plan response is to show your open-minded state by adding this: "We are actively monitoring and analyzing the conditions for this strategy in case a pivot becomes appropriate."

Closing the Deal

To close your deal, your integrity needs to shine brightly throughout your pitch. You have to show investors that you are trustworthy and well prepared for this business venture. Consider these points to help you prepare for closing your investor deal:

- At all times, make sure you are honest.
- Be open about calculated guesses and try to avoid off-the-cuff embellishing.
- Practice your pitch with friends and family, and with a stranger (e.g., a pitch consultant).
- If you don't have an answer, be honest and say that you need to look into that or review your business plan and will have to get back to them.

- Ask how you can best follow up with your investors after they receive your pitch.

This last one is key. At the end of the pitch, you want to have your investors' contact information so you can follow up with them. Give your investor about three days and then contact them to get their thoughts or questions. In this communication, you'll send this message: "I just wanted to follow up and get your feedback, thoughts, and questions on my pitch." Some investors prefer phone calls over e-mail, e-mail over text, or a messaging app over other options. Make sure you know the best way to get in touch with each investor.

Next Steps on Your Journey

As you work through your business launch and the execution of your business plan, remember that you are not alone and that support is always available. If you need professional assistance, I would be glad to work with you on your business plan, strategy development, pitching preparations, and funding needs. Entrepreneurs like you are the heart and soul of what makes our world better every day, and I am so excited for your journey!

Conclusion

Your business plan is more than a document. It is the clarity of your vision. It is the road map to your future, and it is your declaration that you are ready to take meaningful action.

You may find that people take you more seriously when your business plan is finished. They may suddenly "get" your idea now that it's on paper and may tell you how impressed they are with what you are doing. People may even show sudden interest in getting involved and supporting you with their time and money.

Make the most of these new opportunities. With a finished business plan, you automatically create momentum, and things often start falling into place for entrepreneurs at this stage. Sometimes, everything in the business plan begins to materialize as you start following your own plan. Other times, the reality of your path forward is a bit different from what the business plan outlined. Regardless, forward movement is the usual result when your business plan is finally finished.

Next Steps and Help

As you work through your next phases of entrepreneurship, or even if you feel stuck in any part of your business plan, e-mail hello@written-success.co for help. This book is meant to be an aid and a guide, but you may find that you need more support or that you don't have time and want to have a professional build your business plan for you. Written Success can help.

If you are finished with your business plan and need help with funding options, reach out by e-mail to hello@writtensuccess.co to learn about investors, financing, and other funding resources that Written Success works with to help entrepreneurs find the funding they need to start and grow their businesses.

Congratulations, entrepreneur! You are well on your way to fulfilling your business dreams. And congratulations on your success thus far!

Resources

Logo and Branding

www.Ambition.Agency

Ambition.Agency is a provider of high-quality websites, logo designs, and branding materials. Consider them for any new branding or rebranding needs, and tell them Written Success sent you.

Entity Formation

www.hashtag-legal.com

Hashtag Legal is an online legal service provider that creates common-sense solutions for entrepreneurs. If you are interested in learning more about forming your business entity, applying for a trademark, or other legal needs, this team can help you.

Research

https://www.naics.com/search

If you are unsure of what your NAICS code is, you can visit the website above to find your code based on a keyword search.

https://www.census.gov/econ/isp/

The United States Census Bureau's Industry Statistics Portal has great information you can access for free, including visual charts, graphs, and tables that will look great in your business plan. Consider the United States Census Bureau for statistics that show growth or size of your industry, which will be classified and sortable by NAICS industry code.

www.Ibisworld.com

IbisWorld is a great place to learn about the ins and outs of any industry. Search by industry name, type, or NAICS code.

Below are additional sites that are great for digging and researching more into your market:

- Federal Statistics – https://www.data.gov
- U.S. Government Open Data – https://www.usa.gov/business
- U.S. Department of Commerce – https://www.commerce.gov
- Bureau of Economic Analysis – https://www.bea.gov
- U.S. Small Business Administration – https://www.sba.gov/
- Bureau of Labor Statistics – https://www.bls.gov/

Businesses Featured

All businesses referenced in this book are in the start-up phase. Over time, some businesses referenced may change their names, URLs, or business types. For the latest up-to-date contact information on all businesses included in this book, contact Ashley Cheeks at hello@writtensuccess.co.

Learn More about The Vine House

The Vine House is a bed and breakfast built from conception to implementation with a customer-first perspective on one of the nation's most beautiful wine trails in California. For more about booking and planning a stay, visit http://bedandbreakfasttemecula.com/.

Learn More about Kimove

Kimove offers a whole new way to make screen time less passive and more physically and mentally engaging for kids. To learn more about the all-new Kimove brand and for investment opportunities, visit https://www.kimove.com/.

Learn More about TrafficSAMS™ and the Cue Mate

TrafficSAMS™ is a digital variable safety messaging board that increases safety, lowers cost, and maximizes applicability for any walkway, street, or public area. To learn more, visit www.trafficsamsinc.com.

Pool Mate is a company with a line of pool table accessories. The flagship product, the Cue Mate, has received notoriety far and wide for the ingenious design, ease of use, and attractive look.

Learn More about FLO

FLO is a hands-free utility belt designed to anchor on the wearer's center of gravity. This makes tasks such as dog walking safer and more comfortable than other hands-free options. The FLO belt is built from high-quality materials and features a patented 360 ball bearing track for maximum range of motion. For more about the FLO belt, visit www.flodoggie.com.

Learn More about HelloCecil

HelloCecil is a one-way video interviewing software designed for start-ups and small businesses. It was created to allow smaller business teams to execute talent selection and hiring without a robust HR department. HelloCecil is different from other options on the market in both its simplicity and friendly, intuitive interface. To learn more about Hel-loCecil, visit https://hellocecil.com/.

Learn More about TNB Naturals

TNB Naturals is a CO_2 enhancer that bottles the potential to double plant growth and production. Using an all-natural formula and user-friendly application, the practical product is taking the world by storm. For more information about the products, visit www.tnbnaturals.com.

Learn More about Water Elephant

Water Elephant is a healthy convenience store concept with preliminary plans to launch in the Austin, Texas, area. With the purest options available and no tobacco, liquor, artificial colors, or over-processed options, this store will be a place where every consumer can feel great about their visit. For more information about Water Elephant or to connect about investment opportunities, visit www.waterelephant.com.

Learn More about AmaZone

AmaZone Fun Parks (AmaZone USA Real Estate Holdings) is a new theme park chain that is launching in Penha, Brazil, and New York City. It offers the world's largest, most comprehensive indoor replica of the Amazon Rainforest. As an edutainment conservation, AmaZone is the place to learn and enjoy the wonders of the Amazon Rainforest while supporting its conservation. To learn more about AmaZone, visit http://amazonenewyork.com/.

Learn More about CapStratum Management, LLC

CapStratum Management, LLC supports businesses seeking anywhere from $5 million to hundreds of millions in strategic investments. To learn more about CapStratum Management, LLC, visit https://capstratummanagementllc.wordpress.com.

WrittenSuccess
Professional Business Plan Services

Written Success provides business plan and investor pitching services to start-ups and growing businesses. Founded in Houston, Texas, the business services entrepreneurs all over the world.

Entrepreneurs partner with Written Success when they are ready to take their businesses to the next level.

Visionaries, inventors, and disruptors receive one-on-one support to move from idea to action. Traditional businesses learn how to stand out in saturated markets.

Whether the goal is investor funding, bank capital, or strategy refinement, business plan and coaching services are available to support the goals of motivated business owners.

As a partner and coach for several businesses, founder Ashley Cheeks actively helps find areas to monetize, optimize, and achieve full abundance in entrepreneurship for every Written Success client.

Visit https://writtensuccess.co/ to learn more and schedule a free consult.

www.ingramcontent.com/pod-product-compliance
Lightning Source LLC
Chambersburg PA
CBHW071550200326
41519CB00021BB/6676